Wonders of
ITALY

MetroBooks

Wonders of ITALY

Texts
Annie Sacerdoti

Literary coordination
Bianca Filippone

Graphic design
Anna Galliani

Translation
C.T.M.

North American Edition
Managing editor JoAnn Padgett
Project Editor Elizabeth McNulty

CONTENTS

INTRODUCTION   PAGE   12

THE BEAUTY AND THE DIVERSITY
OF THE ITALIAN LANDSCAPES   PAGE   22

A COUNTRY WITH
A THOUSAND CITIES   PAGE   148

FESTIVALS, TRADITIONS AND FOLKLORE
OF AN ANCIENT PEOPLE   PAGE   290

© 1999 White Star S.r.l.
Via C. Sassone, 24 - 13100 Vercelli, Italy
www.whitestar.it

MetroBooks
An Imprint of the Michael Friedman Publishing Group, Inc.

All rights reserved. No part of this publication may be reproduced, stored in a
retrieval system, or transmitted, in any form or by any means, electronic,
mechanical, photocopying, recording, or otherwise, without prior written
permission from the publisher.

This edition published by Metrobooks by arrangement with White Star S.r.l.

ISBN 1-58663-759-2
7 9 10 8 6 4

For bulk purchases and special sales, please contact:
Michael Friedman Publishing Group, Inc.
Attention: Sales Department
230 Fifth Avenue, Suite 700 - New York, NY 10001
212/685-6610 FAX 212/685-3916

Visit our website: www.metrobooks.com

Printed in China

1 The gold, winged lion set in a lunette of St. Mark's Church is perhaps the most famous of the many symbols of the city of Venice, itself one of the most famous cities in the world for its wealth of artistic and natural heritage.

2-3 Courmayeur is a ski resort at the foot of Mont Blanc. A cable car connects it with Chamonix, on the French side, passing over the Aiguille du Midi (one of the most spectacular peaks on the mountain), the Aiguille du Glacier and the Grandes Jorasses (see the photograph).

4-5 The soft morning light strokes the Tuscan hills giving a warm glow to the farmhouses and cypresses scattered throughout the valley. This is Chianti, the region that produces the famous wine of the same name and which is filled with uniquely beautiful vistas.

6-7 The island of Budelli is part of the Maddalena archipelago to the north of Sardinia. Among its many white beaches there is one pink beach formed by coral eroded by the continual movement of the sea.

8 Orvieto cathedral is a masterpiece of Italian Gothic architecture. Extraordinary mosaics and sculptures alternate on the pointed portals and along the façade completed in the 16th century.

9 The façade of Milan cathedral was begun in the second half of the 16th century and finished in 1813. The extension of the spires and pinnacles seem to make the building stretch up to the sky.

10-11 The island of San Giorgio seems to brush St Mark's square in Venice. To the left, the Ducal Palace is an embroidery of elegant and light motifs.

Introduction

Italy has always been "il bel Paese," a beautiful country *par excellence* which the famous medieval encyclopedia created by Pierre d'Ailly described as "the most beautiful country, favorable for the fertility of its soil and the richness of its pastures." Italy was like a dream: "Once you have been to Italy, you will forget other lands. If you have been to Paradise, you no longer need Earth. (...) Europe compared to Italy is like a cloudy day contrasted with a sunny day," wrote Russian writer Nikolai Gogol after a stay in Italy. It is clearly a country that, once discovered, you no longer wish to leave. There is "everything necessary for life and which renders it so delightful," according to Bruzen de la Martinière in the 18th century, and the German poet Heinrich Heine declared, "it is a wonderful thing just to live in Italy."

But what is it that makes Italy beautiful? What is it, seen through the eyes of foreigners, and by those smitten in particular, that has made Italy the ideal setting where one can abandon oneself to pure emotions and violent passions? There are many answers even today and of the

12 The results of the anatomical research carried out by Michelangelo, previously evidenced in the statues of David *(1501) and the* Pietà, *are clearly illustrated in his* Moses *in the church of San Pietro in Vincoli, in Rome.*

13 These famous bronzes are a masterpiece of Greek art; they show two warriors or possibly two kings. They were found in Riace in Calabria and are kept in the National Museum of Reggio Calabria. The artist was certainly of prodigious talent but his identity is unknown; experts have dated the work to 460-450 BC.

14-15 Piazza Navona stands in the heart of Rome. Its oval shape occupies the space once covered by Diocletian's stadium. The square is especially popular after sunset and offers a beautiful all-round view of the three glorious Baroque fountains standing in line and the surrounding churches and palazzi built in the 15–16th centuries which use the ancient stands of the stadium as foundations.

14 bottom Siena, still largely surrounded by its ancient walls, is full of beauty and history. Seen from high up on the outskirts of the city and lit up to show off its most important buildings and monuments, the center of the Tuscan city is resplendent. Easily recognizable are the cathedral and slender bell-tower with its black and white marble bands, and the tall Torre del Mangia.

most varied nature. First, Italy's countryside undergoes enormous variations as one travels from north to south and east to west: within relatively small areas one can see an extraordinary multiplicity of landscapes unfold one after another, sometimes within the space of just a few miles. For example, it is often enough to pass over the brow of a hill or to round the bend of a river to find oneself in completely different natural scenery. When one travels from the mountains to the hills and then to the sea, the contrast is even more obvious. When travelers enter Italy through the Alps, on leaving the peaks and valleys behind, they will be enchanted by the vast lakes at the feet of the mountains. They will be struck by the radiance of the new setting, the pleasantness of the temperate climate and the exuberance of the Mediterranean vegetation.

Visitors who travel the length of Italy will certainly not be disappointed by the magnificence of the hilly scenery through Romagna, Marche and Abruzzi with their thousand hill-top villages like terraces overlooking the long, sandy beaches of the Adriatic coast. They will likewise be captivated by the many islands and marinas that decorate the Tyrrhenian coastline from the Gulf of Naples down to Sicily where the mountains tumble steeply into the sea and the high cliffs are riven by clefts and small bays. The violent beauty of the land is intensified the length of the peninsula by the disquieting presence of volcanic phenomena like the curious blow-holes of Lardarello, the sulphurous baths of Saturnia, the Solfatura of Pozzuoli and Mount Vesuvius in Naples which make the beauty more real.

The coastline, especially in Liguria, made a deep impression on Vidal de la Blanche,

15 top The church of Santa Giustina is one of the oldest churches in Padua. It is unmistakable for its layout in the form of a tripartite Latin cross and for its eight oriental domes that cover the barrel vaults. The original church was built in early Christian times but destroyed by the earthquake at the beginning of the 12th century. The only remains of the building that replaced it are two marble griffins on the façade.

15 bottom The cathedral, the baptistery and Giotto's bell-tower in Piazza San Giovanni are the universal emblems of Florence. The use of green and white marble and chiaroscuro *to lighten the mass of the buildings, together with the daring designs that enabled the dome and bell-tower to be built, are magnificent examples of the engineering skill and imagination of artists like Brunelleschi, Giotto, Pisano and Ghiberti.*

founder of modern human geography, during a trip in 1918. This is part of his description of Liguria: "The mountains stand right over the coastline, one might almost say enveloping it. On the hillsides sloping down to the water's edge, we see the main village emerge from the 'plantations' and olive trees, connected to the beach by stepped paths that are traversed daily by donkeys. Closed between two promontories, stretches out the sandy arc of the shore … onto which the boats are beached."

Italy's rich and varied land is also heavily but harmoniously populated. "The Tuscan countryside simply could not be better kept," wrote Goethe after his trip to Italy, "every clod of earth seems as though it had been passed through a sieve." Indeed, Tuscany, the subject of so many paintings by Botticelli, Leonardo da Vinci and Giotto, seems the perfect example of nature benign to humans and their works, that assists and harmonizes civilization rather than contrasting it. For this very reason, Tuscany is one of the regions of Italy—but certainly not the only one—in which the city-countryside relationship seems especially harmonious, in which these two elements complement one another even aesthetically. The English poet Percy Bysshe Shelley painted an idyllic portrait of Florence describing the city set in a radiant setting which both illuminated it and was illuminated by it. He wrote: "It is surrounded by cultivated hills and from the bridge that crosses the wide channel of the Arno, the view is the most lively and elegant I have ever seen. One can see three or four bridges,

16 top There are thousands of traditions to be found throughout Italy. The carnival masks of Venice are an exhilarating example: the carnival is now a multimillion dollar business for the city which is besieged by tourists from all over the world in February and March who come to enjoy the enchanting atmosphere of the canals.

16 bottom Twice a year, on July 2nd and August 16th, Siena goes wild. The entire population of the city and the surrounding area is caught by the fever of the Palio, the horse race in Piazza del Campo which, in just a few minutes of horses, jockeys and excitement, is the culmination of months of impassioned preparations.

16-17 In Sardinia the Sartiglia, a carnival show dating back to the 17th century, is still a very popular and beloved festival. The main protagonist is the cumponidori, *a masked horseman (accompained by more horsemen contending between them), who is must center a hanging iron star. If he succeeds, peace and health will be enjoyed by all for the following year.*

18-19 *Temple G of Selinunte in Sicily was a building of gigantic proportions (370 x 177 feet) built starting in 530 BC but never completed. It is one of the three temples of which remains are found at Selinunte, the Greek colony which was destroyed and abandoned after a bloody war with Segesta.*

18 top *The Greek theatre of Taormina was in fact rebuilt by the Romans—as can be seen today—on top of the original building and dates from the 2nd century BC. From its cavea in the rock there is a wonderful view over the bay, the city and, in the distance, of Etna.*

19 top The massive pediment of the Temple of Neptune at Paestum frames one of the most impressive temples of ancient times to have survived intact to the present day. It dates back to 450 BC and is one of the numerous important buildings to be found in the archaeological area in Campania enclosed by Roman and Lucan walls from the 4th century BC.

one of which appears to be supported by Corinthian columns, white sails on the boats that stand out against the green depths of the forest that reaches down as far as the edge of the water, and the slopes of the hills covered in every part by splendid villas. Cupolas and bell towers rise on every side and everything is surprisingly neat and clean. On the other side, the Arno valley curves into the distance with hills of olive trees and vines in the foreground, then chestnut trees, and finally one glimpses the smoky-blue pine forests at the feet of the Apennines."

Italy is above all an ancient land with a history of different civilizations that have overlapped, united and been transformed throughout the ages, contributing to give a "cultivated" look to the countryside. Italy is like a large, open history book that details the events of thousands of years, from the rock engravings in Val Camonica to Etruscan remains, from the Greek ruins of Magna Graecia to their Roman equivalents, from Byzantine monuments to glorious Renaissance buildings, up to the present time. To all this should be added a human touch that makes Italy a particularly active and interesting region to all: its folklore, its traditions and its multifaceted popular culture. This is a culture comprising ancient rites transformed and revisited throughout the centuries, that are not "archaeology" but which continue to constitute one of the richest and most appreciated aspects of the soul of the Italian people.

19 bottom Villa Adriana was built near Tivoli between AD 118 and 133 by Emperor Hadrian. He made it into a sort of imperial city which covered an immense area of over 300 acres.

20-21 This aerial photograph shows the large loop of the river Tiber in front of Castel Sant'angelo. Behind the river it is possible to see 16th century Rome, and then past the Forum, the Colosseum and ancient Rome.

The beauty and the diversity of the Italian landscape

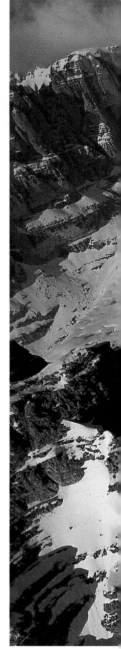

In little more than 116,000 square miles, Italy contains an extraordinary diversity of terrain and nature. In contrast to the permanently snow-capped Alpine and Apennine mountains, there are long coastal strips in Calabria and Sicily that enjoy a temperate-subtropical climate and which are the kingdoms of palm and olive trees. Not far from the large, continental and intensively cultivated Paduan plain traversed by the river Po, stretch broad areas of hills covered with vineyards, and the many north Italian lakes with their own micro-climates. In the south, bare clay valleys, traversed by dry river beds and surrounded by land burnt by the sun, exist alongside the coastal regions with their promontories, flatlands, elevations and valleys. The granite plateaux of northwest Sardinia contrast with the Milanese plain and the gorges of Puglia. Each of these environments, sometimes no more than a few dozen miles from one another, has its own vegetation, colors, sky and light. Combined with the peaks of Sicily and Sardinia, the Alps, that enclose the country to the north, and the Apennines, that run the full length of the peninsular, cover almost 40% of all Italy; of the rest, approximately 20% is flat and 40% is hilly, so, by their very extent, the mountains are an essential part of the Nation. The 620 mile span of the Alps divides Italy from the rest of Europe while the Apennines, running northwest to southeast for 830 miles, cut Italy into two parts. The cut is so clean that it is difficult to pass from the Adriatic to the Tyrrhenian side even though the distance is short.

The forests that cover the Alps and Apennine mountains are Italy's green "lung," but unfortunately they have been decimated over the centuries. Humans have always

22 top The Matterhorn (known as Monte Cervino in Italy) in the Pennine Alps is a little over 14,690 feet high. Its pyramidal shape makes it unique. It dominates the Valtournenche on the Italian side and the valley of Zermatt on the Swiss side.

22 center Mont Blanc (known as Monte Bianco in Italy) is 15,780 feet high and the highest mountain in Europe. Its summit is formed by a succession of peaks and pinnacles and is formed by a number of glaciers.

22 bottom The Catinaccio, or Rosengarten, stands in the eastern Alps between the Fassa and Tires valleys. Its highest peak is the Catinaccio d'Antermoia at 9849 feet. Like the Dolomite mountains, it is formed by numerous pinnacles such as the Towers of Vaiolet.

drawn on these resources without thinking about the future, without considering what would happen once the woods and trees were all destroyed. When the damage caused by deforestation was understood, indiscriminate felling was prohibited and reforestation was introduced but it was often too late. Consequently, the original species of tree was often replaced by another, more resistant, type, conifers in particular, or perhaps species that are not even part of the natural Mediterranean habitat, such as the Australian eucalyptus, that have transformed the natural scenery of many areas.

Italy's mountains have always been inhabited although discontinuously and unevenly. There are still some mountains that have large populations and others that are almost empty. Settlements are often composed of groups of farmhouses, as in Sardinia, or by sizeable villages as in

southern Italy. In these locations, the populations have formed groups since time immemorial to defend themselves from bandits or to escape from malaria which, until after World War II, still existed in swampy areas.

Neither the Alps nor the Apennines have been closed worlds and have never constituted insurmountable barriers to the outside world. Roads, tracks and paths have always cut through them in all directions to allow man to pass. Even if sometimes difficult to use, the crossing points on the mountain passes have always been numerous. Hannibal's army crossed the Alps in 218 BC taking elephants and horses with it; the Romans knew and used seventeen Alpine passes, some of which they built themselves; in the Middle Ages, the barbarians descended on the north Italian plains without any particular difficulty.

22-23 The Brenta Group stands to the west of the river Adda in the eastern Alps. The group is not part of the Dolomites but is considered with them because of the similarity of its bare sides and pinnacles. A lot of ledges mark orizontally the rocky walls, which are deeply eroded by wind and rain. The central part is characterized by true natural architecture works.

24 top The slopes of the Gran Sasso are covered with chestnut trees, oaks and conifers. Higher up, small lakes are commonly found, like Filetto shown in the photograph.

24 bottom The pastures of Gran Sasso are home to grazing animals like this horse in a meadow at the foot of Camosciara in the National Park of Abruzzo.

24-25 The mountain Gran Sasso stands in the middle of the Abruzzese Apennine mountains; its highest peak is the Corno Grande at 9560 feet. Its slopes are covered with vegetation right up to the snowline. Grains and fruits are cultivated on the mountain's sides and cattle, sheep and goats are raised in the meadows for the production of cheese and other dairy items.

Series of foothills slope gently down to the plains from the Alpine and Apennine chains so there is no sudden physical separation of the mountains from the flatlands; on the contrary, the two share an integrated economy. The mountain slopes are used to cultivate grains and fruit while the pastures allow cows, sheep and goats to graze for milk and cheese production. Further up there are mulberries and chestnuts, then oaks and conifers, and finally, where the cold makes vegetation sparse, there are only low bushes, moss and lichen below the snowline. When speaking of mountains, it is natural to think of the highest peaks, Mont Blanc, Monte Rosa, the Gran Sasso or the Maiella and to forget that plateaux and foothills are also included. For example, Lucchesia is part of the Apuan Alps and owes its prosperity to the waters that descend from them but the highest peak there is a little lower than 6500 feet. The mountains in Campania are not restricted to Vesuvius and the Lattari chain that separates the Gulf of Naples from the Gulf of Salerno; they also comprise the area formed by the curve of calcareous peaks at the foot of which are Caserta, Nola and Nocera, and that a rocky spur separates from Salerno. In the foothills of the Alps and Apennines, nature is gentler, the light brighter and the vegetation richer, especially where there are lakes.

25 top left The Apennine mountains in Abruzzo run in successive parallel chains down the Adriatic coast of the region. One of the groups in this section is the Maiella which reaches 9170 feet in height.

25 top right The Sibillini mountains in the central Apennine chain are a watershed between the Tyrrhenian and Adriatic seas. Their highest point is at Mount Vettore at 8123 feet. At the feet of these mountains, wide plains open out where a carpet of brightly colored flowers appears as soon as the snows melt so that they are in full flower at the start of summer.

Italy abounds with lakes, many of which were created by the actions of glaciers during the Quaternary period. The largest number of lakes is found at an altitude of 5900—9180 feet in the Alps: there are over 400, some of them large like Misurina near Cortina d'Ampezzo which is over half a mile long, and others small, like the Blue Lake in Valtournanche at the feet of the Matterhorn and lake Carezza in the heart of the Dolomites. Lakes are the dominant feature in

two areas in Italy: at the foot of the mountains between Piedmont and Veneto, and in the volcanic zone between Lazio and Campania.

Lake Orta, or Cusio, as it was called by the Romans, is the westernmost of the pre-Alpine lakes and lies entirely in Piedmont. It is perfectly sized: small enough to be seen all at one glance but also large enough to contain all the natural features of the larger lakes, even if on a smaller scale. On the island of San Giulio in the middle of the lake stands a church dedicated to St. Julius.

Lake Maggiore, or Verbano, spreads across the boundary between Piedmont and

Lombardy. It covers 80 square miles and is 1220 feet deep. One of its shores is in Swiss territory. The lake is fed by the Ticino and Toce rivers and is connected to Lake Lugano by the river Tresa. The overall shape of the lake is complex; it receives an abundance of water from the mountains that keeps the vegetation luxuriant on the steep slopes that tumble into the water and around the little bays and pebbly beaches. Villa Taranto, near Pallanza, and Villa Pallavicino, near Stresa, are two of the magnificent residences with Italian gardens that hosted aristocrats and nobles from all over the world until the 19th century.

Floating just in front of Stresa, the three islands of Borromeo are like precious gems set in the water. Palazzo Borromeo and its Italian garden stands on Isola Bella; the original village with its twisting alleyways is built on Isola dei Pescatori; and in the center of its park on Isola Madre there is a 16th century palace that has been transformed into a botanical garden for exotic plants and flowers. These are favored by the mild climate and sheltered by the surrounding mountains. The lakes of Monate, Comabbio, Biandronno and Varese are situated near to the southern bank of Lake Maggiore; they were formed in the same manner and at the same time as their larger neighbour. Lake Como, also known as Lake Lario, is in Lombardy. The surrounding mountains alternate steep, tree-covered gorges with shores lined with gardens and flowers. It covers 56 square miles. The lake was loved by author Alessandro Manzoni whose novel, "I Promessi Sposi," was set here. The northern tip is separated from the main body of the lake by the bottleneck at Colico; further down, the lake forks at Bellagio, one stretch leading to Lecco and the other to Como. Lake Como is fed by the Mera river and the Adda, the second of which continues its journey at Lecco. During the 19th century it was chosen to be the seat of country residences for aristocratic families. Still standing today between Como, Tremezzo and Bellagio are some of the most beautiful mansions built on any of the lakes, all of them boasting extensive Italian gardens: Villa d'Este, Villa Pliniana, Villa Serbelloni and Villa Carlotta. Lake Iseo, or Sebino, is formed

by the river Oglio running down from Valcamonica on its journey across the Po Valley. This Lombard lake boasts the largest lakebound island in Europe, Montisola, flanked on either side by two tiny islets, Loreto and San Giorgio. A few miles from the lakeshore at Cislago, there stand what the locals affectionately call the "wood fairies." These are extraordinary natural towers of earth and stone each topped by a large rock so that it looks a little like a hat. These "pyramids" have been created by the erosive forces of water washing away the surrounding soil to leave the towers standing up to 98 feet tall.

Further east we find Lake Garda, called Benaco by the Romans. The river feeding it from the north is the Sarca which changes its name to the Mincio when it leaves again from the southern shore. It is the largest lake

27 bottom In the center of Lake Maggiore, in front of Stresa, are the three Borromeo islands (Isola Bella, Isola dei Pescatori and Isola Madre) like jewels set against a backdrop of intense colors.

in Italy, covering 143 square miles, and it is almost considered a sea especially by the Austrians and Germans who are frequent visitors there. Because of its size, the various shores of Lake Garda are very different. They are lined with castles (like the Scaliger forts at Sirmione and Malcesine), sumptuous villas (like Villa Bettoni at Bogliaco on the Brescian side or Villa Albertini at Garda on the Veneto side) and gardens of Mediterranean vegetation (oranges, lemons, citrons, olives and vines are grown on its banks thanks to its extremely mild climate but also exotic plants as in the Hruska botanical garden at Gardone Riviera). The lake touches on three regions: Lombardy to the west, Veneto to the east and Trentino to the north east. The Sirmione peninsula, so loved by the Roman poet Catullus, stretches out into the lake on the south shore separating the two gulfs of Desenzano and Peschiera.

26 top Paleological finds have shown that Lake Como has been inhabited since time immemorial. Its strategic position between Italy and Switzerland has made it a transit point for centuries on the descent to the Po Valley.

26 bottom On the island of San Giulio, in the center of Lake Orta, stands the church of the saint of the same name. A 15th century bas-relief tells the story of the miracle of his arrival on the island which was infested with snakes and monsters at that time. When Julius spread his cloak on the water, it turned into a raft. On reaching the island, he cleared it of the unfriendly creatures and built the church. This episode marked the beginning of his life as a preacher.

26-27 During the 19th century, Lake Como was chosen as a place to holiday and relax by the aristocracy and beautiful residences were buit. The picture of the small port of Pescallo with its boats at anchor is typical of the tranquillity of this lake, still a popular holiday destination.

27 top The waters of Lake Garda lap onto the territories of three regions: the western side is in Lombardy, the eastern in Veneto and the northeastern in Trentino. Its shores differ markedly from one another but all boast castles, like this Scaliger stronghold at Malcesine.

28 top Lake Bolsena in Lazio (left) fills the main crater of the volcanic area in the Volsini mountains. Two islands sit in the center of the lake, Martana and Bisentina. Lake Corbara (right) in Umbria is surrounded by old farmhouses and acres of meadows.

28-29 Lake Vico in Lazio fills the crater of the volcanic Cimini mountains. The shores of the lake are surrounded by ancient forests.

29 top Lake Trasimeno in Umbria has no outlet. It is shallow and fed only by rainwater. For centuries it has been a center of meditation and is surrounded by Franciscan and Benedictine monasteries.

29 center The houses of Anguillara Sabazia face onto Lake Bracciano in Lazio. The name either derives from eels (anguille) that live in great numbers in its waters or from the aristocratic family, Anguillara.

29 bottom Algae and aquatic grasses are harvested in Lake Posta Fibreno in Lazio which are dried and used for cattle feed or fertilizer.

Lake Trasimeno is the largest lake in central or southern Italy. It was formed by floods and tectonic action and is fed by no river; it is shallow and the waters are supplied almost exclusively by rain so that its level is subject to extreme alteration from one year to the next. In the 15th century, Fortebraccio da Montone, the nobleman of Perugia, tried to dig an outlet from it to the Nestore basin but to no avail. The lakes' flat sides lined with poppies and marsh grasses have been the sites of many battles, the most famous of which was in 217 BC when the army of the Carthaginian general, Hannibal, overcame the Romans. The battle was so cruel that it is still recalled today in local place names: Sanguineto (bloody), Ossaia (charnel), Sepoltaglia (burial ground). Moving further south, close to Rome, another lake district is found with an unusual formation. These lakes exist in dormant or collapsed volcanic craters on Mounts Volsini, Cimini and

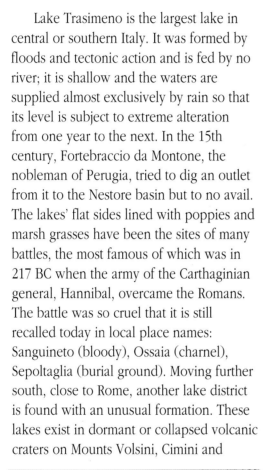

Sabatini and in the Alban hills. The lakes are named Bolsena, Vico, Bracciano, Albano and Nemi. Romans visited them frequently for their proximity to Rome, especially during summer when the heat becomes unbearable. They built castles and country residences or they went, just as they do today, for outings. The surrounding countryside is of fields, vineyards and pastures for the many herds of sheep. Different surroundings are to be found at the two coastal lakes, Lesina and Varano, on the edges of thick forest on the Gargano promontory in Puglia. These are more lagoons than lakes. Lesina is separated from the sea by a strip of land half a mile wide and is only 5 feet deep; it has brackish water and is infiltrated by the sea. Varano is Italy's seventh largest lake and separated from Lesina by Mount Elio, a small hill on which prehistoric remains have been found.

Sicily is a separate world from the mainland although its mountains are, from a geological point of view, a continuation of the heights of Calabria despite being on the other side of the Strait of Messina. Sicily's northern chain is divided into various groups: the Peloritani, the Nebrodi and the Madonie which are all in fact part of the same structural unit. Along the north west side of the island, the mountains of Palermo that surround the Conca d'Oro extend as far as Trapani with similar features: they are calcareous and dolomitic massifs from the Mesozoic period, mainly isolated, that overlook gently sloping clay and sandstone hills. The center of the island is a succession of undulations interrupted by Mount Cammarata (5177 feet) and ten or so other peaks (all over 3280 feet) which form the Sicani group of mountains between Corleone and Cammarata. In all directions as far as the Mediterranean there is a sea of modest mountains and valleys: to the east as far as the Erei, to the northeast as far as the Madonie, to the north as far as the

Busambra rock, and to the west as far as one of the euphemistically named "Montagna Grande" (the last western peak in Sicily, to the west of Calatafimi, and just 2460 feet high).

In ancient times the island was covered with forests of chestnut, oak and beech trees except for the coasts, the alluvial plains and the more recently created lava areas. All eastern Sicily is dominated by Mount Etna which, with good reason, can be considered a world apart from the rest of the island. It is a huge mass of black lava and tufa which contrasts vividly with the snow white peak and the green vegetation of its slopes. It is the largest active volcano in Europe and one of the largest on Earth. It is formed by a central cone and two hundred groups of occasionally active small side cones able to spew forth fluid lava which can then spread for huge distances.

The terrain of Sardinia is completely different to that of the Alps, the Apennines or Sicily. Arriving by sea, then moving inland, the visitor soon realises that this is a very unusual mountainous environment made up of isolated massifs—Gallura, Nurra, Gennargentu, Iglesiente and Sulcis—connected by plateaux of different heights and environment or by variably sized tectonic depressions such as those of Campidano and Cixerri. The long geological history of this island, more similar to France than to Italy, has shaped it into an utterly original environment. Its elevations are the result of the tectonic dislocation of an ancient granite massif which has been gradually smoothed over the centuries by erosion.

30 top The large Campidano plain in Sardinia stretches from the bay of Oristano to the bay of Cagliari and separates the Inglesiente-Sulcis mountains from the hills of Trexenta and Marmilla. It is a typical tectonic depression bordered by faults sometimes in the shape of rounded hills like those at Pula (see photograph) and hot water springs, like those at the spas of Sardara and Villasor.

30 center The huge mass of Mount Etna dominates eastern Sicily. Its flanks were once covered by copses of chestnut and oak trees and broom.

30 bottom The visitor in Sardinia is often confronted by bare, treeless countryside as far as the eye can see, like this one at Barbagia.

30-31 The Sinni is one of the few rivers that run through Basilicata. It has its source on Mount Sirino and runs through a long valley before reaching the bay of Taranto near Nova Siri 58 miles later. The rivers in this region— the Bradano, the Basente (the longest at 95 miles), the Cavone, the Agri and the Sinni—are all torrential rivers, i.e. they are powerful during the winter rains but nearly dry during the summer drought.

32 Portofino promontory is a nature reserve that sticks out 2 miles between Paradise and Tigullio bays. Portofino is a famous corner of Liguria for its natural beauty, the multicolored houses that surround it like a ring and for the richness of vegetation on the hill behind it.

32-33 Oltrepò Pavese occupies the huge province of Pavia from the right bank of the river Po east to the border with Emilia and west to the border with Piedmont. In all it covers 425 square miles. The vineyards that produce the famous red wines, Bonarda and Barbacarlo, are the most characteristic feature of the

countryside of rounded hills topped by old villages, many of which hold works of great artistic value. Agriculture is the main income producing activity (besides wine, cereals and livestock are produced) but there are also factories operating in the food, textile and iron and steel industries.

33 These three views of the different sections of the Italian countryside show the diversity of the country's landscapes: Argentario (top) used to be an island but has now become a promontory with typically marine flora; Garfagnana (center) is mountainous in the center gradually giving way to hills; the Po Valley (bottom left) is utterly flat and this province, Vercelli, is flooded for many months of the year for the cultivation of rice.

Italy's flatlands are not so extensive as either the hill or mountain areas and cover only approximately 20% of the country. These are nearly always alluvial valley formed by detritus deposited by rivers over millennia. The most important and the largest, covering 70% of Italy's flatlands, is the Po Valley through which the river Po and its tributaries run. The Po Valley has been greatly transformed by man during his history in north Italy. Its forests were cut down to make room for agricultural land, it was divided up into lots and several marshy

areas have been drained. The northern section of the plain is calcareous so that water is easily drained into the subsoil but the southern section contains layers of clay which does not let the water pass and creates pools on the surface. This is the so-called "springs" strip which divides the drier areas cultivated with cereals and vines from the "wet" zones used for rice and irrigated meadows. This farming area stretches from the tip of Veneto in the east to Emilia Romagna in the south west and has been profoundly altered by man in his slow transformation of nature. The same process has taken place in other small plains throughout the mainland and the islands: for example, on the Tyrrhenian side of the Apennines there are the lower Arno valley and Maremma in Tuscany, the Roman countryside in Lazio and the plain in Campania; on the Adriatic side there are the tablelands of Puglia and the zones around Bari and Otranto; in Sicily there is the Catanian plain and in Sardinia, the Campidano. Italy has 5360 miles of coastline, half of which are represented by Sicily and Sardinia. The Ligurian coast starts at the French border and is divided into the eastern and western rivieras by the Gulf of Genoa. At its deepest point, the Ligurian sea reaches 9180 feet. The western riviera is covered with olive groves and greenhouses which are not only attractive to look at but represent a huge industry.

From Ventimiglia to Genoa, the coastline is made up of sandy beaches separated by promontories with terraced hills behind. From Genoa to La Spezia on the eastern riviera, the scenery changes: the coast is high and rocky with frequent coves and projections like the Promontory of

Portofino which encloses the Gulf of Tigullio, or the point at Porto Venere which ends the bay of La Spezia. This stretch of coast has one of the richest vegetations in Italy and the maquis on the Portofino promontory is protected.

The coastline that runs down Tuscany and Lazio (from La Spezia to Rome), to where the river Tiber reaches the sea, resulted from alluvial formation. The Tyrrhenian coast is low with sandy ridges, called "tomboli" in Tuscany and "tumoleti" in Lazio, which create coastal pools like those on the Orbetello promontory. This zone typically consists of maquis along the coast itself with a long strip of pine trees behind, at one time quite dense. Some of this area, like the Maremma, used to be marshland but were drained at the start of the century. Just off the Tuscan coast stand the islands of an archipelago of which the largest is Elba. They too are covered with typical Mediterranean flora but unexpectedly lush for its geographical position. This is due to climatic conditions (high temperature, clear skies, little rain) more akin to Naples or Palermo than Pisa or Livorno.

34 top The coastline of Terracina on the bay of Gaeta boasts a wide sandy beach. The town of Terracina stands at the feet of the Ausoni mountains at the edge of the Pontine plain near the Roman road, the Via Appia. It is both a fishing port and an agricultural center besides being a seaside resort. From the hill where the remains of the temple of Jove Anxur are found, there is a wonderful view over the Circeo promontory and the islands of the Pontian archipelago.

South of Rome, what was once a large swamp is today a highly cultivated area of Lazio. The Pontina plain has kept some of its original coastal lagoons at Sabaudia, Fogliano, Caprolace and Monaci and offers a natural environment that is unique to the mainland: there is an area of dunes covered with maquis, lakes behind (as in Circeo park), with forests of oak, ash, hornbeam and elm, mixed with eucalyptus. From Circeo promontory to the Cilento peninsula, the coastline forms a series of arcs to create the gulfs of Gaeta, Naples and Salerno.

The Ponziane islands sparkle in the sunshine in front of Gaeta while the islands of Ischia, Procida and Capri are in the Gulf of Naples. This is where the Tyrrhenian sea, maximum depth 12,240 feet, is the dominant theme in the local scenery with its range of intense blues. All the hillsides here are terraced with orange, lemon, fig and almond trees and vegetables and flowers which have replaced the original maquis.

The rather squat Cilento peninsula has its furthermost point at Cape Palinuro, where a species of primrose grows that dates back to the Tertiary period. This is followed by the Policastro gulf, with its high coastal land, and the two Calabrian gulfs of Sant'Eufemia and Gioia. Here the beaches are low and sandy in short stretches. The Strait of Messina is only 2 miles wide. It is the body of water that connects the Tyrrhenian sea to the Ionian, that washes the long Calabrian and Pugliese coasts as far as Santa Maria di Leuca and the Strait of Otranto, where the Adriatic begins. The Ionian coast is high and rugged with mountains that fall straight into the sea and furrowed by river beds that are dry all summer and which rage after the winter rains. There are few ports in this area dominated by the gulfs of Squillante to the west and Taranto to the east. Across the wide Salentina peninsula and Puglian tablelands, the countryside changes completely. The coast of the Adriatic sea (which only reaches a maximum depth of 3953 feet) is straight and has few ports due to its geological formation. The Gargano peninsula is the only projection, bordered by coastal lakes

and confronted by the Tremiti islands. Mount Conero stands on the coast overlooking the port of Ancona. North of Ravenna we find the stretch of low, marshy coastline, lagoons, islands and cane-brake in the valleys of Comacchio and in the wide Po estuary. These are continued in the lagoons of Venice, Marano and Grado which have been greatly transformed by the hand of man. After the Gulf of Venice, the coast is flat and traversed by a series of parallel rivers as far as the Gulf of Trieste where the rocky and jagged coastline is covered in a wealth of vegetation.

34 center The crags of Pizzomunno in Puglia, eroded by the action of water and wind, stand out boldly in front of the cliffs on the shoreline. They are without doubt among the most fascinating creations of the sea erosion.

34 bottom The three famous crags of Capri in the Bay of Naples rise massively out of the water; their round bases rise to pointed tips on a horizontally layered column.

34-35 Amalfi stands in the center of the Amalfitana coast which stretches from the Bay of Naples to the Bay of Sorrento. Today Amalfi is a tourist resort and fishing port but in the 8th-9th centuries it was a sea-faring republic. The main part of the town is centerd around the port; the houses in the typical Campanian style are generally colored white or in pastel shades. The roofs are built

to an ancient design that allows rainwater to be collected and acts as insulation against the heat. The coast is dotted with more colored houses, Saracen towers and citrus orchards. The view from the coast road over the clear waters of the sea is simply stupendous and, in the air, the Mediterranean smells of rosemary, oregano, strawberry trees, honeysuckle, cluster pines and holm oaks linger.

36 top The island of Vulcano is part of the Eolian archipelago and lies off the north of Sicily. Its name is a clear indication of its origin: it is formed by a crater with three cones that are still active. Near to the Gran Cratere, a depression more than 500 yards in diameter, the Piano delle Fumarole can be seen from which sulphur vapours escape continually. Legend has it that the island, called Thermessa in ancient times, was the home of Eolo, the "lord of the winds."

36 center Lampedusa is the largest island in the Pelagian archipelago and is closer to Tunisia than Sicily. The Isola dei Conigli in the photograph is a favorite place for sea turtles to lay their eggs.

36 bottom Cape Teulada is the southernmost point in Sardinia between Sant'Antioco and Cagliari. The history of Sardinia influenced the look of the island itself: the towers built along the coast in Medieval times were used as lookouts against attacks by Saracen pirates.

36-37 The Maddalena archipelago, to the north of Sardinia and between the coasts of Palau and nearby Corsica, comprises seven islands: Maddalena, Caprera, Santo Stefano, Spargi, Budelli, Santa Maria and Ràzzoli. The magnificent island of Budelli (see photograph) has some of the best beaches of the whole group. Its coral depths color the sand and give the waters that bathe the island the transparency of a tropical lagoon.

Once again the two large islands, Sicily and Sardinia, are worlds unto themselves. The high and rocky Tyrrhenian coast of Sicily is lined with gulfs; nearby the Eolian (or Lipari) volcanic islands of which two, Stromboli and Vulcano, still host active volcanoes. Other islands, like Ustica to the west near Palermo, and the Egadi group at the western tip of Sicily, are like small gems set around the larger island. Sicily's southern coastline is completely unlike the others. It is flat with slight curves and washed by the shallow Sicilian sea (only 5416 feet deep) with Pantelleria and the

Pelagian islands not far from the coast. The western coast faces onto the Ionian sea and is split into two: the center opens onto the Gulf of Catania while the north is straight.

The Sardinian shores are very different: jagged to the northeast with rocks eroded by the wind and, not far away, the Maddalena archipelago; with the wide Gulf of Cagliari on the south side, facing the islands of San Pietro and Sant'Antioco; and high on the long western coast that faces Spain.

38 top Classic and alluring, this view of the Dente del Gigante shows how the vertical layering of the granite, combined with the effects of wind and water, have created a sort of jagged monolith.

38 bottom The Aiguille Noire spears the soft white clouds which partially cover the south crest. Mistakenly considered a "minor" pinnacle on Mont Blanc, it is and always has been one of the most elegant and sought after peaks by mountain climbers.

THE SPLENDOR
OF THE PEAKS

38-39 The enormous bulk of Mont Blanc, is here seen from the wall of Freney, recognisable by the large glacier where the Bonatti expedition made its dramatic attempt at descent in 1961.

39 top left The contrast between the intense blue sky and the whiteness of the ice of the Grandes Jorasses, seen from Courmayeur, enhances the magnificence of these famous peaks which, at over 13,120 feet, dominate the central section of the Italian-French border behind Val Ferret.

39 top right The summit of Mont Blanc, rightly nicknamed the "King of the Alps," was climbed for the first time in 1786 by Balmat and Paccard.

40-41 The Courmayeur side of Mont Blanc; on the left we see the top of the mountain, on the right the Brenva wall is clearly identifiable. A little lower down, it is possible to see a part of the Brenva glacier whose southern tip stretches toward Val Veny.

42 top Valsavarenche is one of the six tributary valleys that feed into the Dora Baltea river from the south side. It is covered with woods of beech, maple, linden and pine trees and, on the increase, spruce and larch. Crowning this thick vegetation are the snow sprinkled peaks.

42-43 The region of Valle d'Aosta is enclosed by the Graie and Pennine Alps. It covers over 1,150 square miles, many of which are covered permanently by snow and ice, like the walls of extraordinary mountains like Mont Blanc, the Matterhorn and Mount Rosa.

43 top left It is not unusual to find glorious scenery at the foot of Mont Blanc like the one in the picture. The small church at Entrèves, a stone's throw from Courmayeur, shyly peeps over the snow dunes while the amphitheatre of mountains behind makes for one of Europe's most spectacular settings.

43 bottom left The village of La Thuile stands at 4,728 feet on the French border in the extreme north-west of Valle d'Aosta on the road that leads to the Colle del Piccolo San Bernardo. La Thuile is not just famous for its summer and winter tourism but also for the presence of layers of anthracite in the rock nearby.

43 right Pointed like the church spire, the unmistakable trunk of the Matterhorn, Monte Cervino to Italians, rears up against the blue of the sky. The massive block of granite 14,691 feet high was climbed for the first time in 1865.

44 top *The ibex, a hoofed mountain mammal, owes its survival in Europe to the creation of the Gran Paradiso national park. The last specimens not to have been hunted or poached were able to increase in number in the protection of the park and now this magnificent creature has been returned to much of the Alps.*

44 center *The Monviso massif stands in the Cozie in the western part of the Piedmont Alps. It features a series of peaks, the highest of which is the Bric di Monviso at 12,600 feet. It overlooks the Po valley and is the source of the river.*

44 bottom *The national park of Gran Paradiso can be reached by road either from the south in Piedmont or from the Valle d'Aosta valleys to the north, like Valle di Rhêmes in the picture. Chamoix are one of the two hoofed species that live in the park where they are protected like the rest of the fauna and flora.*

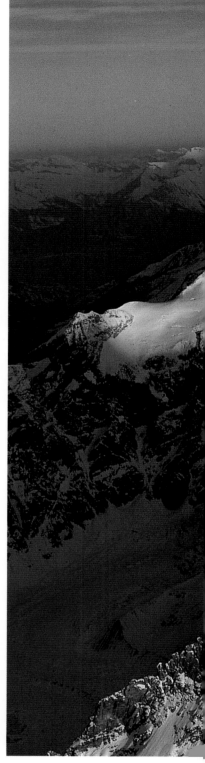

44-45 *The aerial photograph shows the unique and stunning outlines of the Matterhorn in the foreground, the mountain that rises over Cervinia, on the Italian side, and Zermatt, in Switzerland. Mont Blanc can be seen in the background.*

45 bottom The National Park of Gran Paradiso covers the Graie Alps on the border between Piedmont and Valle d'Aosta. It was established in 1922 and protects many species. There are roughly sixty glaciers in its 280 square miles.

46-47 The massif of Mount Rosa stands on the border between Valle d'Aosta and Piedmont. The highest observatory in Europe is found on Gnifetti Point. Although the peak is tinged with pink at sunset (rosa is Italian for pink), the name comes from a German term—the area has many ancient walser sttlements—which means "glacier."

48-49 Two parallel valleys run down the side of Mount Rosa that overlooks Valle d'Aosta: Valle d'Ayas (see photograph) is the western of the two. Its wider spaces than the Valle di Gressoney to the east have made it one of the most popular summer and winter tourist destinations.

49 top left The medieval Fénis castle is probably the most resistant to the rigours of the weather in Valle d'Aosta. It was built from 12th–15th centuries near the village of the same name in the Dora valley. Still standing are the solid rectangular towers, the more slender circular tower and the crenellated walls.

49 bottom left Heading down the valley toward Aosta, the ruins of the castle of Châtelard can be seen near La Salle. The best preserved section is undoubtedly the tall circular tower which stands out against the snow-topped Mount Berrio Blanc.

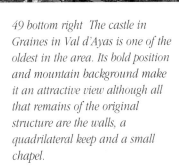

49 top right Aosta is the capital of the smallest region in Italy. The town was founded by the Romans during the reign of Augustus and called Augusta Praetoria; it still retains some ruins from that period. It was built near the river Dora where the valley opens out, in a position that favored human settlement and a point of communication.

49 bottom right The castle in Graines in Val d'Ayas is one of the oldest in the area. Its bold position and mountain background make it an attractive view although all that remains of the original structure are the walls, a quadrilateral keep and a small chapel.

50 top left The district of Alagna comprises a number of smaller, decentralized administrative areas. The traditional wooden houses scattered around the Alpine valley have covered balconies or loggias for drying and storing hay.

50 bottom left Bardonecchia, close to the Fréjus tunnel, is one of the most fomous winter sports resort in the province of Turin.

50-51 A thick white blanket covers the walser style houses in Alagna, in Valsesia. This style was brought to the valley at the foot of Mount Rosa by people moving south from the Swiss valleys.

51 top left Limone Piemonte stands in the southernmost area of "Granda," the province of Cuneo, in Val Vermegnana. A famous tourist resort in the Maritime Alps, Limone can boast a fine Gothic church built in the 14th century.

51 top right One of Piedmont's top winter resorts, Sestrière was built by the Agnelli family in the 1930's. During the summer, the mountain is wrapped in thick foliage but in winter, it changes its covering to the white cloak that attracts thousands of skiers.

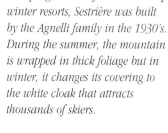

50 top right Sestrière takes its name from Lapis Sixtra, the milestone placed sixty miles from Turin. The town's main income is earned from winter skiing. The resort in the Val di Susa held the World Ski Championships in 1997.

50 bottom right The fairy-tale, white snowed Rimasco, in Val Sermenza, rises next to a tributary of the river Sesia.

52 left Near the boundary between Lombardy and Trentino-Alto Adige in the central Alps, stands Mount Cevedale in the Ortles group. Glaciers and the effects of glaciation from the Pleistocene epoch are common to the whole massif.

52 top right The typical wooden houses of Livigno along the town's main road dot the snow covering the valley of the same name. Livigno is situated near the Swiss border at a height of 5,900 feet in a Customs-free zone.

52 bottom right The river Adda runs through Valtellina, the valley that divides the Ortles group of mountains in its upper stretch, then separates the Retiche Alps on the northern side from the Orobie Alps to the south further down. It is one of Lombardy's largest valleys covering over 1500 square miles.

52-53 Mount Presanella, 11,666 feet, is one of the peaks that make up the Adamello range in Trentino-Alto Adige. The Tonale Pass, is the point at which one passes into the Val di Sole on the northern side. Areas of Mount Presanella are permanently snow-covered.

53 bottom left The Bernina range of mountains on Lombardy's border with Switzerland is made up of a series of peaks around 10,000 feet high. One of these, Pizzo Roseg at 12,913 feet, is shown in the photograph. Rifugio Martinelli stands in the foreground at an altitude of 9,228 feet.

53 bottom right Situated at a height of 4,000 feet at the extreme northern end of Valtellina, Bormio is both a winter sports resort and a spa. Historically, its fortune was linked to those of the Visconti and Sforza families; today, traces of its noble past are still evident.

54 top left Any view of the Cima della Tosa is breathtaking. The mountain, seen here tinged with pink against the evening sky, has been smoothed from the effects of wind and rain.

54 bottom left The Brenta range next to the Dolomites is seen in this bird's-eye view. This is a favorite destination for courageous climbers that love venturing into its highs and glaciers.

54 top right The play of light and shadow on the Crozzon di Brenta emphasizes its natural beauty. The horizontal layers typical of the Dolomites and the Brenta group are clearly seen although, strictly speaking, the Brenta is not part of the Dolomite chain.

54 bottom right Cima della Tosa takes its name from its resemblance to a shaved head. It stands 10,335 feet high at the southern tip of the Brenta range.

55 The warm light of sunset plays on the jagged surfaces of the Brenta range. Situated west of the river Adige, it anticipates the shapes and colors of the Dolomite mountains further east.

56-57 The tenuous colors of the evening light are projected onto the Torri del Vaiolet in the Catinaccio range. The three peaks that form the chain are named after the climbers who first scaled them, Delago, Stabeler and Winkler.

56 bottom left The Catinaccio range rises immediately west of the Marmolada group and appears a rocky bastion closed to exploration.

56 bottom right The Catinaccio is also known as the Rosengarten, or garden of roses, from a local legend in which King Laurino lived in a magnificent palace on top of the mountain; the palace was covered in roses which threw their reflection throughout the valley.

57 top The landscape of the Pale di San Martino is unique and the environment so precious that the National Park of Panaveggio-Pale di San Martino has been created to protect it. The Pale plateau is a sort of rocky desert at an altitude of over 4,500 feet.

57 center Sunset weakens the glare of the snow and gives the Cimon delle Pale an unreal air. Molded by the constant action of the glaciers, wind and rain, the pinnacles of Pale di San Marino have taken on extraordinary shapes.

57 bottom The rocks of the Piz Boé lit up by the evening light separate the intense blue of the sky from the brilliant white of the snow.

58-59 The Sella group o f mountains is bounded by Val Gardena to the north and Val di Fassa to the south. It seems like a set of natural amphitheatres created by glaciers. The summit of the massif is a long plateau that contrasts strongly with the surrounding peaks.

60-61 The stratification that makes the Dolomites so unusual is clearly visible in this picture of Mount Cristallo. Snowfalls leave white streaks on the irregular walls of the rock that give off a light of rare beauty when caught by the sun.

60 top left The Dolomites are a range of mountains that have been shaped by the weather into pinnacles, towers and massive walls of rock riven by clefts and channels. The snowline lies at roughly 9,000 feet.

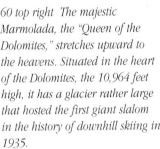

60 top right The majestic Marmolada, the "Queen of the Dolomites," stretches upward to the heavens. Situated in the heart of the Dolomites, the 10,964 feet high, it has a glacier rather large that hosted the first giant slalom in the history of downhill skiing in 1935.

61 top left Piz Boé, 10,338 feet, is one of the most characteristic peaks that stand over the cylindrical mass of the Sella group. To the south, the massive rock walls slope down to Val di Fassa, on one side, and to Livinallongo, on the other, to create a splendid natural setting.

61 bottom left The Tofane triad, known as the "three sisters," is the pride of the Ampezzane Dolomites. The highest point is the Tofana di Rozes. The summit of this 10,580 foot high peak seems to be irregularly encircled by a group of rock pillars.

61 top right The Sassolungo (literally "long stone") is the symbol of Val Gardena. Seen from the valley road, it looks like a huge "stone."

61 bottom right The spectacular walls of the Sella range offer skiers and climbers excellent opportunities to test their abilities on challenges of all grades. An unbroken chain of lifts allows skiers to ski around the Sella without removing the skis from their feet.

62-63 Some shepherds in Valle del Senales in Trentino-Alto Adige still practize a type of nomadic cattle breeding, the transhumance, by transferring their flocks from Italian to Austrian pastures by crossing glaciers such as this one, the Similaun. The practice, however, has almost died out.

62 bottom and 63 top Droving flocks is not a simple logistical exercise but rather a seasonal ceremony in which the whole family takes part.

Days of preparation are required in which the flock is brought together, the animals branded and their condition checked.

63 center The droving is long and tiring, constantly under the guidance of the shepherd who controls the movement of the animals, especially in the more difficult sections. The sheep have to deal with all types of terrain, including rock, snow and ice.

63 bottom The aid of the sheepdog during grazing and droving s absolutely necessary. On the snow-covered peaks, the dog carries out his tasks like a true professional and his understanding with the shepherd is perfect.

64 top The summit of Sass Pordoi seen from the Sella pass is shown covered in passing clouds. The 9,685 foot Sass Pordoi is one of the outer peaks in the Sella group which, in this part of the southern face, looks onto Pordoi pass.

64 center The brilliant colors of the dense Alpine conifers contrast with the pallor of the jagged Dolomite rocks, which stand against a blue sky.

The wonderful divergence in colors and shapes is captured in this photograph taken from the Antermoia valley.

64 bottom The red, orange and ochre colors of sunset cover the Sasso delle Nove, in Val Badia, in a remarkable light. The play of light on the dolomitic rocks never fails to produce a breathtaking effect, particularly as evening draws on.

64-65 Wandering over the paths in the Dolomites, it is not unusual to come across settings that induce a moment of contemplation, like this one on Alpe di Susi with its marvellous view over the Sassolungo.

65 bottom left Mount Pelmo rises like a rocky dome in the area of Cadore at the eastern end of the Dolomites. Cadore, which was the theatre of a bloody revolt during the Risorgimento (the

uprising of the Italian people against Austrian domination), winds along what is now the border between the regions of Veneto to the west and Friuli-Venezia Giulia to the east.

65 bottom right During the coldest time of the year when the evergreens stand out against the white background, the view of the majestic and solemn Sassolungo is a stirring sight as it points its wrinkled profile to the evening sky.

66 top left The bell-tower of the church in Ortisei, holiday resort in Val Gardena, is topped by a peculiar spire commonly found all over Tyrol.

66 bottom left Val Badia is one of the valleys that cleave the Altoatesine Alps. There are corners here unspoilt by man and with centuries old vegetation that are an oasis of peace.

66 right The church of St. Oswald was originally built in the 14th century and rebuilt a century later. It is the most interesting building in Sauris di Sotto, a small village in Friuli–Venezia Giulia. The top of the bell-tower is onion-shaped and rests on an octagonal drum.

66-67 The Sasso Nero as against the background of the Castello di Tures. Originally built in the 12th century but altered many times since, this splendid bastion that dominates the Aurina valley seems to come from a fairy-tale.

67 bottom left The mansi are typical of the eastern Alps. These buildings are linked to grazing and the word mansi is no more than a distortion of the medieval Latin word mansum.

67 bottom right Under the brush-strokes of a thick snowfall, Fusine lake washes against a part of the forest of Tarvisio, a natural environment of extraordinary value.

68-69 and 69 bottom left The bright green of the conifers contrasts with the warm tints of the hay-fields. In Val Badia, as in all Alpine valleys, agriculture has always gone hand in hand with livestock farming.

68 bottom Val Gardena in Trentino-Alto Adige is where vegetation reigns unquestioned. All shades of green are present in a patchwork of extraordinary beauty.

69 bottom right At the access to the plateau of Alpe di Siusi, a small town has been transformed into a popular tourist destination: Castelrotto, whose church of St. Michael can be seen in the photograph, stands at an altitude of little more than 3,280 feet, surrounded by attractive scenery.

69 top left Near Livinallongo, the white buildings scattered over the meadows stand out against the emerald slopes. With the approach of summer, the Alpine countryside bursts into all hues of green.

69 top right Cortina d'Ampezzo is without doubt the Alpine holiday resort par excellence. It is equipped with superb winter-sport facilities but is also popular in summer for its panoramic setting and because it is an excellent starting point for treks of all grades of difficulty.

70 top Villa Pallavicino is one of the magnificent residences to be admired at Stresa, the town on Lake Maggiore famous for luxury tourism. The building stands inside a private park beside the lake.

70 bottom The enchanting Borromeo islands lie in Lake Maggiore. A small village stands on Isola dei Pescatori, in the foreground, over whose roofs can be seen the bell tower of the church of St. Victor. Palazzo Borromeo and its Italian style garden are situated on Isola Bella, seen here in the background. There is also a larger, third island, Isola Madre.

FRESHWATER REFLECTIONS AND DROPS OF LAND

70-71 Angera is a small Lombard village on the southern shore of Lake Maggiore. It owes its fame to the Fort which has a splendid view over the lake. The imposing construction was originally built for defense purposes but was later converted into a residence by the Borromeo family.

71 top left The village of Orta opens onto the lake of the same name. In front of the village lies the island of San Giulio with its austere church dedicated to the saint. The story goes that the construction of church was actually started by the saint himself.

71 top right The snow-topped mountains of Verbano act as a background for the patrician villas of Orta which lie next to the turquoise waters of the lake.

72 bottom right The village of Malcesine stands on the northeastern shore of Lake Garda. The tiny islet dell'Olivo lies just in front of the well-preserved center. Like many other local places, Malcesine has lived through turbulent periods, passing among the hands of the della Scala and Visconti families, and the Veronese and Austrian powers.

72-73 The Scaliger castle at Sirmione, spa town on Lake Garda, was built at the end of the 13th century for defense purposes. Its angular towers, with Guelph (swallowtail) or Ghibelline (square) crenellations, makes it particularly attractive. The castle, on the narrowest part of Sirmione peninsula, is almost entirely surrounded by water.

72 left Two boats bob in the port of Desenzano, a tourist town on Italy's largest body of freshwater, Lake Garda.

72 top right The unconventional genius of Gabriele d'Annunzio is well represented by his house-cum-mausoleum, the Vittoriale degli Italiani, that the poet built on Lake Garda and lived in from 1921 to his death. The open-air theater in the large garden is just one of the parts of the complex that d'Annunzio built to celebrate himself.

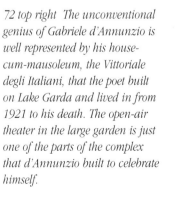

73 top This is the minuscule harbor at Malcesine, on Lake Garda known as Benaco by the Romans. The village stands at the feet of Mount Baldo and was an integral part of the Scaliger defenses that wound along the lake shores.

74-75 There are many wonderful villas surrounded by beautiful parks on the shores of Lake Como, also known as Lake Lario. One of the more appreciated decorative elements in such parks is the cypress tree. It is usually possible to reach these villas by boat which are moored by a waterside entrance.

75 top left Ossuccio is a small village on the shore of Lake Lario in front of Isola Comacina. The gracious Romanesque church of St. James stands just outside the pleasure-boat harbor.

75 bottom right Bellagio is the pearl of Lake Como and stands on the promontory formed between the two forks. This attractive situation has prompted the construction of many aristocrats' villas. Standing in the old center is the Romanesque St. James's church, restored at the start of the 20th century. The bell tower is seen against the background of Tremezzo on the other side of the lake.

75 bottom left The nice holiday town of Iseo is situated on the southern shore of Lake Iseo. The lake, known by the Romans as Sebino, runs for 15 miles along the Brescia-Bergamo provincial border.

75 top right This is the view from Brunate hill in one of the southernmost points of Lake Como. The lake is in the shape of an upside-down "Y" with the western fork running down to the town of Como and the eastern fork to Lecco.

77 center The solid-looking castle of Doria di Passerano in the province of Asti was eventually finished after a series of attempts between the 14–16th centuries.

77 bottom A superb 14th-century castle stands at Pozzolo Formigaro in the province of Alessandria, once the dominion of the marquis Del Bosco.

78-79 Long lines of vines run parallel across the rounded hills turning the land to all shades of red, yellow and green. La Morra, in the photograph, is one of the largest wine production zones in the area. Several delicious wines are produced here of which the best is Barolo.

RICE FIELDS AND VINES

76-77 Wines from Monferrato such as Barbera, Grignolino and Freisa are known around the world. The picture shows vineyards alternating with cultivated fields and woodland near Ottiglio where the church stands out among the hoses of the center.

76 top left Vicoforte stands among the gentle hills in the middle of a plateau at the feet of the Maritime Alps. The hilly countryside embraces the Vicoforte Sanctuary whose dome was designed by the famous architect from Mondovì, Francesco Gallo.

76 top right The hills of Monferrato, between the river Po and the Ligurian Apennines, seen in the early morning in a mixture of warm, almost autumnal, hues.

77 top Near Magnano, on the Serra di Ivrea, the Romanesque church of St. Secondo stands in a beautiful frame of fields.

80 top left In spring, the rice-fields are flooded and the countryside around Vercelli seems like a huge lagoon divided into sections by earth banks. Here and there, "grangias" (traditional and self-sufficient rural enclaves) and the occasional poplar tree stand out of the waters like a sort of mirage.

80 bottom left Casalrosso, a small farming center south of Vercelli, is reflected in the rice-fields below an unquiet sky. The first buds on the trees and the flooding of the fields indicate that the picture was taken in late March or early April.

80 top right The river Sesia flows down from Mount Rosa on its way to the river Po. Its winding course marks the border between the provinces of Vercelli, to the west, and Novara, to the east. Its course often creates small sections of marshy land called "lame" that are home to wetland birds. Some of the river's waters are diverted to flood the rice-fields in spring.

80 bottom right Pavia in Lombardy is identical to Vercelli in Piedmont as far as rice cultivation is concerned. Around Bereguardo, the many rice-fields turn bright green in late spring with the growth of the new plants.

80-81 The snowy peaks of Mount Rosa stand over the Vercelli plain, whose main cultivation is rice. Before the introduction of sophisticated machinery, cleaning parasites out of the rice was done by labourers. Today it is rare to see them; their work has been replaced by mechanical and far less evocative methods.

81 bottom The golden yellow of the ears shows that the rice is mature and ready for harvesting. This stage of the cycle takes place between August and October. The grains are separated from the remains of the plant and the skin, then treated and sold. Rice, originally from southeast Asia, is the main contributor to the economy of the Vercelli area.

82-83 The last rays of the sun to the west seem to set the flooded fields on fire. When the fields are flooded, the countryside around Vercelli is often surreal.

84 top The gently undulating land below Mount Dolada and Mount Cavallo in eastern Veneto form the hills of Marca Trevigiana.

84 bottom The Euganean hills to the south of Padua are home to several famous resorts. One of them, Battaglia Terme, includes several stately villas surrounded by gardens and parks.

A LAND GENTLE
BY NATURE

84-85 Bassano del Grappa is situated on the southern edge of the Sette Comuni plateau in a strategic position that has determined its fortunes over the course of history. The present attractive center is composed of the original medieval town and the Renaissance palaces surrounding it. Bassano also boasts a wooden bridge, Ponte Coperto, over the river Brenta. Following several alterations, its present design is probably the work of Andrea Palladio.

85 top left Little of the castle built by the barbarians in Conegliano Veneto can be seen in the recently altered version. The building is now the home of the Civic Museum.

85 top right It is not rare to find fields of sunflowers in the area of Trevigiano, the area near Treviso. As the position of the flowers tells us, the photograph was taken from the south.

86 top and bottom left One of the many islands in the lagoon near Venice is the island of Burano, originally a fishing village. The houses are brightly colored to distinguish the separate properties clearly. Like Venice, the island is crossed by canals suitable for small boats.

86 right Two islanders are engaged in mending their nets, still a fundamental chore for the inhabitants of Burano.

86-87 Seen from above, Burano is like a speck of land in the waters of the lagoon. The bell tower stands over the brightly painted houses while tiny harbours and open land line the edges of the island. In the distance, the island of Torcello can be seen.

87 top left Close to Burano, Torcello boasts some of the lagoon's most interesting buildings: primarily the cathedral of Santa Maria Assunta with its impressive bell tower visible miles away to those who arrive by ferry. The church was founded in 639

but underwent a series of alterations in the 9th and 11th centuries. The simple façade denotes the division of the church into three naves. The huge windows along the sides of the church illuminate the interior with natural light.

87 top right The island of St. Francis in the Desert is the greenest in the lagoon. The name is derived from the belief that Francis stopped at the island on his return from the East. The religious buildings and brilliant coloring of the cypress trees give the island a particular attraction.

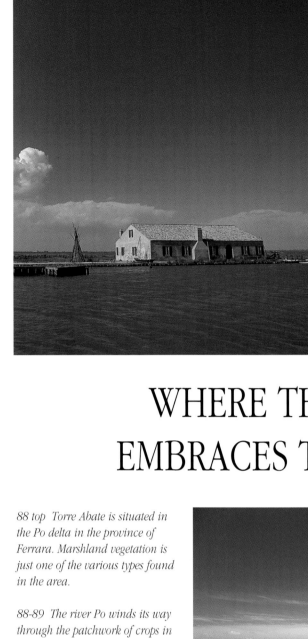

89 center Small fishing boats are moored near Scardovari in the Po delta. The water is stiller where the river meets the sea and is suitable for the breeding of mussels.

89 bottom A fisherman patiently prepares his tools on the waters of Gorino valley.

WHERE THE PO EMBRACES THE SEA

88 top Torre Abate is situated in the Po delta in the province of Ferrara. Marshland vegetation is just one of the various types found in the area.

88-89 The river Po winds its way through the patchwork of crops in the valley it gives its name to. The river terminates in a wide delta as it flows into the Adriatic sea. Continuous formation of sandy creeks pushes the delta roughly 76 yards further into the salt water each year.

89 top An old fishing house seems to emerge from the waters of the Comacchio valley. This area in the province of Ferrara, south of the Po valley, has been largely drained over the last decades.

90 top The picture shows the sailing school of San Fedele in the well-known resort of Albenga midway on the riviera between Genoa and the border with France.

90 center A narrow strip of sand separates the sea from the houses of Noli, a small tourist resort south of Savona.

90 bottom Noli boasts several small artistic treasures like the 13th-century municipal tower and the castle. A large 11th-century circular tower stands inside the walls of the lather.

A CLIFF CRESCENT-MOON FILLED WITH THE SEA

90-91 Like many Ligurian towns and villages, Laigueglia, situated next to Alassio, used to be a trading town in the 12th and 13th centuries. Now, its mild climate and lovely position mean its main income is from summer tourism.

91 top left The breaking waves on the beach at Varigotti leave a rim of white foam. Although the beaches of Liguria are usually narrow and rarely sandy, this region has always been popular with tourists.

91 top right Varigotti seems to hide in the shelter of a rocky outcrop. The picture shows the multi-colored houses, the almost deserted beach and the coastal vegetation climbing among the rocks.

92 top left The extreme tip of Portofino promontory, coated in green mediterranean vegetation, stands out on the background of numberless inlets.

92 bottom left The old, pastel-colored houses of Portofino frame the square, a natural stage that slopes gently down to the harbor. The lovely, three-nave church of Portofino can be seen in the background.

92 top right San Fruttuoso is a minuscule Ligurian village on the slopes of Mount Portofino. It can only be reached by boat, then by climbing a mule track. The village is not only attractive for its position but also for a lovely monastery built by Prospero, bishop of Tarragona, who fled to Italy after the arrival of the Arabs in Spain, bringing the ashes of the saint with him.

92 bottom right Since the English consul, Montague Yeats Brown, bought Portofino fort in 1845, many members of the jet-set have followed him. There are many splendid villas hidden among the trees owned by artists, sportsmen, film stars, politicians and aristocrats.

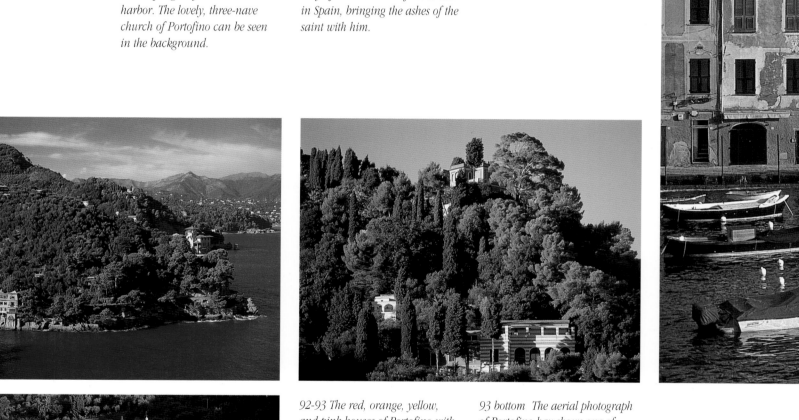

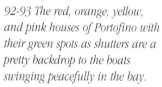

92-93 The red, orange, yellow, and pink houses of Portofino with their green spots as shutters are a pretty backdrop to the boats swinging peacefully in the bay.

93 bottom The aerial photograph of Portofino bay shows one of Italy's most popular destinations for international jet-setters. The yachts belonging to the rich and successful float peacefully on the blue velvet of the sea.

94-95 One of Italy's most exclusive resorts, Portofino, is situated on a promontory that looks out to sea on one side and over the protected harbor on the other. The renovated houses that line the beach made up the original fishing village and are perhaps better cared for than the large and expensive villas built on the promontory.

96-97 *A ferry prepares to leave the port of Camogli north of Mount Portofino. Camogli was made famous during the 19th-century by its commercial shipping fleet but the industry failed when technology progressed beyond the limited experience of the shipowners; today the local economy is based on tourism.*

96 bottom left *Hundreds of pleasure boats crowd the marina of Santa Margherita Ligure, one of the most chic resorts on the Ligurian coast. The old palazzi along the sea-front have been turned into elegant shops, restaurants and cafes.*

96 bottom right *Painted wooden boats are drawn up on the beach of Camogli safe from the breaking waves.*

97 top *The 16th century castle of Rapallo sticks out to sea, only connected to land by a small stone road from the port. The fortunes of this town have always been linked to the rivalry between Pisa and Genoa to such an extent that, without adopting a position that would have limited its freedom, it made enemies of both cities and suffered retaliation from both.*

97 center *The island of Sestri Levante has been joined to the mainland by an embankment that also created a cosy little harbor. The sheltered beach, the climate and pretty views have made Sestri a popular seaside resort.*

97 bottom *The houses in the old quarter of Priaro around the harbor of Camogli are tinged with the colors of sunset.*

98-99 Portovenere is a beautiful medieval town on a strip of land south of La Spezia. Of particular note are its city walls and the recently restored, 12th century church of St. Lawrence.

98 bottom left Manarola is the most picturesque of the Cinque Terre, the five villages situated precariously on top of cliffs that drop sheer into the clear sea waters.

98 bottom right Vernazza is another of the Cinque Terre, situated between Monterosso al Mare, to the north, and Corniglia, to the south.

99 left Vineyards around Manarola have used the terrace system for hundreds of years. The grapes grown here are used to produce the Cinque Terre wines and the famous Sciacchetrs.

99 top right Riomaggiore is the administrative center of the Cinque Terre, the five fishing villages linked by that name.

99 bottom right The Cinque Terre are linked by a railway line dug out of the rock and seemingly suspended over the turquoise sea.

THE HEART OF ITALY, NATURALLY

101 top right Turrite Secca on the banks of the river Turrite is a village in the heart of Garfagnana, a lovely area of green slopes between the Apuan Alps and the Apennines.

102-103 The Tuscan Maremma is a fragile ecosystem protected by a nature reserve. Here one finds many species of trees lorded over by the sinuous trunks of the Corsican pine.

100 top Legnaro is an inland village in southern Liguria just beyond Monterosso. The bell tower of its small church stands out against Punta del Mesco.

100 center The Apuan Alps are part of the foothills of the Tuscan Apennine mountains. Their particular color is created by the marble content of their rock.

100 bottom The Abbey of St. Antimo, near Montalcino in the hills of Siena, was founded in the 9th century by the Benedictines but only the Romanesque church, renovated in the 12th century, remains.

100-101 The clear bell tower of Castelvittorio rises over the red roofs clear against the backdrop of hills.

101 top left Due to the clay content near Volterra, and the consequent landslides that such terrain is subject to, the hills here become very steep.

104 top Known world-wide for Brunello, a delicious wine made from a single type of grape, the Sangiovese, Montalcino stands on the slopes of the Orcia valley. The fortunes of Montalcino were always held in balance between the forces of Siena and the Medici family in Florence.

104 bottom One of the Medici's most splendid villas was built at Poggia a Caiano, a few miles from Florence. Giuliano da Sangallo was commissioned to build it by Lorenzo the Magnificent. The villa was enlarged and further decorated by Pope Leo X and renovated once more in the 19th-century.

104-105 Sorano, a few miles from the border between Lazio and the Tuscan province of Grosseto, still shows its medieval layout. The turrets in the warm colors of the local stone and the Ursinea Fortress look out over the lovely Lente valley.

105 bottom left The Castle of Four Towers was built in the 14-15th centuries in the hills near Siena. The tall cypress trees that surround it are a typical feature of the most appreciated Tuscan landscape.

105 bottom right The countryside of Tuscany is sprinkled with villas built by the Medicis where the Florentine nobles liked to relax. One of them is the Villa La Peggio near Grassina which was bought by Francesco I de' Medici in 1569.

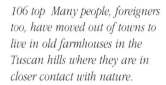

106 top Many people, foreigners too, have moved out of towns to live in old farmhouses in the Tuscan hills where they are in closer contact with nature.

106 center The province of Siena is not just a land of vines and olive trees: the green fields that cover the gentle hills provide rich grazing for sheep.

107 center and bottom
The farmhouses and the tracks that connect them to the rest of the world stand out clearly against the open stretches of grass, the cultivated fields and the cypresses of the Tuscan hills.

106 bottom *The low clouds seem to touch the soft grassy blanket that covers the rises and falls of the valley whereas a group of cypress trees carelessly casts its shadow to the ground. This is Orcia valley, one of the prettiest areas in central Italy.*

106-107 *A white, beaten track, like many in the Orcia valley, winds through a meadow. On either side, the cypress trees line the passage right up to the farmhouse.*

107 top *There are many country villas in the Tuscan hills like this one in Radda in Chianti. In this area, they are often surrounded by long rows of vines which produce the famous Chianti wine.*

108 top Capraia is an island of volcanic origin in the archipelago off the coast of Tuscany. The vegetation is scarce and the rocky coast is lined with grottoes and creeks.

108 bottom Portoferraio, preferred port of entry to the isle of Elba, lies on the north coast. The Tuscan island is the largest in the archipelago and the third biggest in Italy after Sicily and Sardinia. Elba depends almost entirely on tourists who go there to appreciate the wild Mediterranean maquis, a clean sea and a semi-tropical climate.

108-109 The tower of the Castle of St. George points up against the blue sky over Capraia. The Tuscan island, known by the Romans, is interesting for its geological formation: basalt, tufa and andesite combine to form this speck of land.

109 center The picture shows the port on Giglio island, also part of the Tuscan archipelago. Thick Mediterranean vegetation and a blue sea are the main features of this island that lies opposite the Argentario promontory.

109 bottom The ecosystem of the Uccellina mountains on the coast south of Grosseto has been protected from man by the creation of a nature reserve.

109 top The Argentario promontory extends into the Tyrrhenian sea in the southernmost part of the province of Grosseto. This strange geographical feature combines the attraction of the mountain with that of the sea that laps against its jagged rocks.

110 top left Umbria is often defined as the green heart of Italy. The picture of the horses under an olive tree was taken near Ferentillo in Valnerina.

110 bottom left The ochre of an isolated farmhouse stands out against the green countryside of Umbria.

110 top right Trevi dominates the valley of Spoleto. In Roman times the town was called Trebiae.

110 bottom right The waters of the Marmore waterfall bounce from one surface to another in the luxuriant vegetation. The waterfall was created artificially during the 3rd century BC by bringing the waters of the Velino and Nera together to prevent flooding.

111 The harmony of the Umbrian countryside near Trevi is created by a group of elements: winding roads, parallel rows of silver-leafed olive trees and low, long farmhouses wrapped in the brilliant foliage of the surrounding trees.

112-113 The Sibilline mountains stretch along the border between Umbria and Marche. This area of the Apennines is particularly suitable for summer grazing. From May to September, all kinds of grazing animals live on the slopes of the Sibillines where they find plenty to eat throughout the summer.

112 bottom left Seen from afar, Spello appears like a brush-stroke over the verdant Umbrian countryside. The narrow lanes, Roman remains and Renaissance buildings of Hispellum, as it was known to the Romans, certainly merit a visit.

112 bottom right The soil of Umbria not only supplies typically Mediterranean fruit and vegetables but products with a foreign flavor—like tobacco in this plantation near Todi.

113 top left In the woods close to Assisi stands Eremo delle Carceri. This place was chosen by St. Francis and the members of his Order as ideal for meditation and prayer. Originally just a small church and caves, the site was later enlarged till it reached its present size.

113 bottom left A slight mist envelopes of Corbara and covers the artificial lake. The colors are attenuated by the morning dew giving the countryside a surreal atmosphere.

113 top right The area around Cereto di Spoleto, a village at the feet of the Umbrian Apennines, is one of the most attractive in the region for its exuberant flora.

113 center right Looking out from Spello over the surrounding countryside, the eye can wander at will over the unending meadows, woods, olive groves and solitary farmhouses.

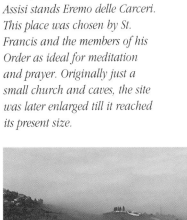

114 top left Cocullo is a small village in the province of L'Aquila built over the remains of the Roman town of Coculum on the southern face of Mount Catini. The tower of its medieval castle dominates the houses from its position in the center of the village.

114 bottom left At an altitude of 4,100 feet, the village of Opi in the upper Sangro valley falls within the boundary of the National Park of Abruzzo.

114-115 The Corno Grande, here standing over an immense expanse of yellow flowers, is the highest peak of the Gran Sasso. The massif even has a small glacier, the Calderone, the most southerly in Europe. The Corno Grande is not just the highest summit in the Gran Sasso but the entire Apennine chain.

115 top The National Park of Abruzzo, opened in 1923, was the first of its kind in Italy. Besides the brown Marsicano bear, the park also protects the Abruzzo chamois and other species.

116-117 The village of Castelluccio, the highest in the Sibilline mountains, stands on the snowy slopes of Mount Vettore.

114 top right On the strip of Lazio that sticks out between Umbria and Abruzzo there is the Terminillo, a mountain standing 7,260 feet high popular with winter sports lovers.

114 bottom The National Park of Abruzzo includes highlands such as Mount Marsicano which is snow-covered all year round.

118 top The photograph shows an attractive view of some buildings on Ventotene, one of the Pontian islands. The handrail of a stairway zigzags against the orange of the walls and green of the window shutters.

118 bottom Like the other islands in the Pontian archipelago situated off Gaeta bay, Ponza is of volcanic origin. The soil consists of tufa and andesite and the jagged rocks fall sheer into the sea.

GREEN PROMONTORIES AND SHINING BAYS

118-119 Cap Bianco (white cape) is a small section of the coastline on the island of Ponza. Its white rocks drop vertically into the crystal clear waters.

119 top left Ponza is the largest inhabited center on the island of the same name. The traditional activities of agriculture and fishing are now supported by a flourishing tourist industry.

119 top right On the west coast of the island lies the Bay of Chiaia di Luna where the luminescent white rock contrasts strongly against the dark sea.

120 top left The isle of Capri seems to float on a blue velvet cloth. When seen from above, the island appears to be an extension of the Sorrento peninsula seen in the distance. Capri's unmistakable cliffs can be seen on the southeast coast of the island.

120 bottom left The famous Blue Grotto is to be found at the extreme north of Capri.

120 top left The port of Gaeta is situated on the north side of the peninsula that extends into the Tyrrhenian sea. The town has many beautiful monuments and buildings, both civil and religious. Its name is supposed to be derived from the Roman Caieta.

120 bottom right Piazza Umberto I, framed by the white houses with vaulted or terraced roofs, is the center of daily life on Capri.

120-121 At the foot of Mount Solaro in the highest part of Capri, the village of Anacapri is bathed by sunshine. This tourist resort, with its breathtaking views, can be reached by road or by cable-car.

121 top Sperlonga lies halfway between Terracina and Gaeta. Some of its medieval walls are still standing and, not far away, the remains of a Roman villa have been found—possibly the private residence of Emperor Tiberius.

122-123 Fishing has always been the traditional activity at Procida, the island in the gulf of Naples situated between Cape Miseno and Ischia. The nets are hung out in the sun and mended by hand.

122 bottom The harbor in the town of Ischia is situated in the most recently built quarter, Ischia Porto. The harbor is always busy and welcomes tourists wanting to take the waters in its spa or simply to enjoy the climate and beautiful sea of the largest island in the gulf of Naples.

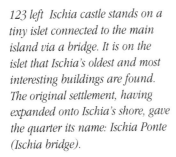

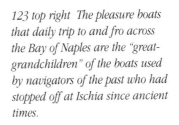

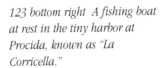

123 left Ischia castle stands on a tiny islet connected to the main island via a bridge. It is on the islet that Ischia's oldest and most interesting buildings are found. The original settlement, having expanded onto Ischia's shore, gave the quarter its name: Ischia Ponte (Ischia bridge).

123 top right The pleasure boats that daily trip to and fro across the Bay of Naples are the "great-grandchildren" of the boats used by navigators of the past who had stopped off at Ischia since ancient times.

123 bottom right A fishing boat at rest in the tiny harbor at Procida, known as "La Corricella."

124-125 The photograph shows the extraordinary view of the Amalfi coast taken from the terrace at Villa Rufolo in Ravello. The luminous blue of the sky is reflected in the sea that gently laps the jagged rocks.

124 bottom The Amalfi coast is a breathtakingly beautiful section of the Tyrrhenian shoreline where traditional activities, such as fishing, have been progressively supported by tourism. Visitors first arrived in the area during "Grand Tour" days.

125 top left and center The majolica tiles and eastern shape of the dome and bell tower on the church at Praiano are similar to those on the Church of the Assumption in Positano. The white houses of Praiano on the Amalfi coast are surrounded by the colors and smells of the Mediterranean maquis.

125 bottom The clear terraced houses and the Church of the Assumption slope steeply down to Positano beach. The village, north of Cape Sottile, used to be only a fishing village but now it is one of the most well-known tourist resorts on the Amalfi coast.

125 right The environmental and geographical features of the Amalfi coast are unique. The sheer, white limestone outcrops, marked with brightly colored plants and flowers, make the shoreline most unusual.

126-127 The beach at Vieste, Gargano's largest town, is a huge expanse of sand that slips into the turquoise water. The medieval section of the town still exists around the castle built in those times.

126 top The Gargano promontory is surrounded by one of the loveliest seas on the Italian coast. The rocky spur on the "boot" of Italy extends west of Tavoliere della Capitanata.

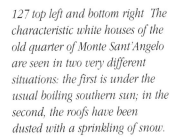

127 top left and bottom right The characteristic white houses of the old quarter of Monte Sant'Angelo are seen in two very different situations: the first is under the usual boiling southern sun; in the second, the roofs have been dusted with a sprinkling of snow.

127 bottom left The unmistakable white and gray cones of the trulli are some of Italy's most celebrated constructions. Ancient dwellings originally from the Megalithic period, trulli are perhaps related distantly to the nuraghe of

Sardinia. The small houses in Puglia are usually circular; they are topped by a false, dry dome (i.e., not using cement or other binding materials) which is either plastered or lined with strips of wood.

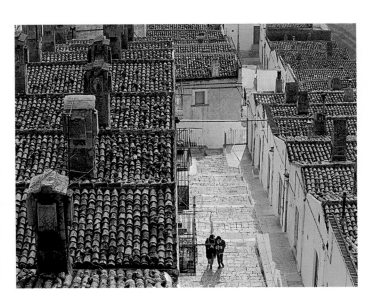

127 top right The white houses of Ostuni spread over three hills to the north of Brindisi. In the past, the town was subjected to the domination of various powers, the last of which was the kingdom of Spain until 1806.

128 left This unusual columnar basalt rock formation is found in the Gole dell'Alcantara, a river that enters the sea near Taormina in Sicily. The prisms of rock have been revealed by the erosive action of the water on lava.

128 top right The Madonie, limestone and dolomitic higths in northern Sicily, are covered with a thin layer of snow. The massif is not quite 6,561 feet in height and owes its name to the surrounding ancient fiefdom, Madonia.

A STONE'S THROW
FROM AFRICA

128 bottom right The rows of vines and grass fields near Alcamo in northwest Sicily cover the countryside like a chessboard.

129 Red hot lava flows down the sides of Mount Etna. Symbol of Sicily, the mountain is both loved and feared. The volcano gradually emerged from the sea roughly 500,000 years ago.

130 top left Fishing boats are drawn up on the beach at Cefalù on the north coast of Sicily. Traditionally a town that earned its living from the sea, it is now a popular holiday resort.

130 bottom left Fishing boats wait their turn in the harbor at Favignana on the largest of the Egadi islands. The island lies off Trapani and gets its name from the Favonian wind which favors the fishing of tuna.

130 top right This spectacular aerial photograph clearly shows the two arms of land that extend from Taormina to the sea. They are Cape Taormina, left, and Cape Sant'Andrea, right.

130 bottom right Santa Tecla, near Acireale, is a picturesque village made from stones of lava. In the distance, majestic, snow-covered Etna dominates the countryside.

130-131 Capo Bianco on the Sicilian coast: the transparency of the sea, the whiteness of the limestone rocks and the wide sandy beach make this a small paradise.

131 bottom The ancient Greek city of Tindari and the salt lakes, formed by the action of the sea on sand, create an unreal landscape.

132-133 *A Bronze-Age village has been discovered on Cape Milazzese on Panarea in the Eòlian islands. This site archaelogical is particularly attractive as it is almost surrounded by the sea.*

132 bottom *The immaculate houses of Panarea contrast with the thick vegetation and unusually leaden sky. The island lies halfway between Lipari and Stromboli and is a paradise for snorkellers and divers.*

133 top Stromboli, the northernmost of the Eolian islands, is dominated by the volcano of the same name. Several small villages, like Ficogrande in the photograph, exist on the island, but all on the eastern side of the mountain where no damage has ever been caused by eruptions.

133 center and bottom The unspoiled coast of Panarea is lined with bays and coves. Bare rocks are ranged along the shore in a precise aesthetic order, like a shower of small meteorites fallen from space.

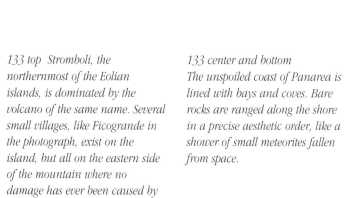

134 left Lampedusa is the closest island to Africa in the Pelagian chain. It lies over 125 miles from Sicily but its southern coast is very near to Tunisia.

135 top Cala Pozzolana is a beautiful sheltered cove on the island of Linosa. The northernmost island in the Pelagian chain, Linosa is of volcanic origin and almost completely uninhabited.

135 bottom Lampedusa was abandoned for a long time but repopulated in the second half of the 19th century. Today its port is filled with dozens of yachts year round.

136-137 Salina is the second largest of the Eolian islands for population and size. Its luxuriant vegetation makes an attractive contrast with the cobalt blue of the sea. Its mountain, Mount Fossa delle Felci, stands 3,126 feet high.

134-135 Cala Madonna is one of the inlets that surround the coast of Lampedusa. The clear water laps a mass of limestone that is almost wild.

134 bottom Isola dei Conigli, near to the southern coastline of Lampedusa, is a marvel of white beaches and clear blue water. It is one of the loveliest places in the south of Europe.

138 top The Giara di Gesturi is a wild plateau in the heart of Sardinia that is home to a number of animals extinct elsewhere, for example, the small Sardinian horse with its long mane, which still lives wild here.

138 center Collection of rainwater in a region where rain is scarce has always been a problem. Lake Cedrino in Barbagia is an example of how the Sardinians have attempted to take advantage of torrent water for irrigation purposes without harming the environment.

WILD LAND,
ENCHANTING SEA

138 bottom The huge Pula plain to the south of Cagliari is an example of the amazing variety of landscapes that Sardinia has to offer. The visitor will be surprised at the riot of color and Mediterranean vegetation in the meadows to be found inland on an island seemingly so barren.

138-139 Lula in Sardinia is surrounded by a bare and wild mountainous countryside. The ridges are part of Mount Turuddu and the limestone rocks of Mount Albo. The verdant and lovely landscape might almost belong to the Dolomites.

139 top left The unusual morphology of the Marmilla in central-southern Sardinia is shown in the picture. The remains of a 12th-century castle on a pyramidal hill dominates the flat land roundabout.

139 top right CastelSardo takes its name from an ancient fort originally called Castel Genovese and built by the Dorias in 1102. When the Spaniards from Aragon governed the island, its name was changed to Castel Aragon but the castle was given its current name under the Savoyard regime in 1769.

140-141 The sandy beaches to the north of Palau on the Emerald Coast are protected by dunes that burst into color in spring. The roots of the flowers and plants that grow there are essential to hold the sand together.

140 bottom The Costa Smeralda (Emerald Coast) and Sardinia's northern side in general boast beaches with pure coral sand and clear water the equal of any tropical island.

*141 top right and center
The Gallura coastline is jagged,
riven with inlets and often fronted
by islands. Lookout towers are
often to be found on the mainland,*
*like that of Longosardo near Santa
Teresa. Santa Reparata bay, like
those of Porto Quadro, Marmorata
or Conca Verde, offers views over
a sea of enchanting beauty.*

*141 left and 141 bottom right
The land around the promontory
of Cape Testa is unique and
spectacular. Due to the continual
erosion of the reddish granite
from wind and water, the rocks
overlooking the sea have been*
*carved into the strangest shapes.
The granite caves opened by
the Romans in this area can still
be seen; they left large square
blocks of granite that have now
been smoothed over the
centuries.*

142 top left Unusual rocky formations fall into the sea at Nebida bay in Iglesiente. The "Sugarloaf," a large limestone crag, can be seen in the center of the photograph.

142 bottom left Porto Pino in Sulcis takes its name from the large pinewood that used to surround the bay, one of the largest in the region. The 24 acres that have survived the ravages of men and time represent one of the last natural pinewoods in Europe. Large dunes of the whitest sand separate the vegetation from the sea along the coastline.

142 top right In Iglesiente, the morphological features of the land, the wind and the tiny grains of sand plucked from the sea have created an African landscape. Huge dunes are in continuous movement along the edges, and sometimes invade, the vegetation.

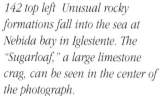

142 bottom right A colony of pink flamingos has nested on Molentargius cove, just outside Cagliari, over the last few years. This is an important but not unusual event in Sardinia which is on the routes of many migrating birds.

142-143 Cala Viola is a splendid sandy beach bounded by exuberant vegetation in the inlet between the capes of Argentera and Caccia. The name comes from the wine-colored land, the Sardinian verrocano, a mixture of ancient rocky sediments.

143 bottom The Bay of Chia, in the center of the southern coast, is a palette of colors with the green of the uplands, the white of the rocks and the green-tinted blue of the water. The lookout tower, a not unusual sight in Sardinia, dominates the marvelous countryside.

144 top The Maddalena Archipelago in the north of Sardinia offers countryside of great beauty:pinnacles of granite and twisted rock alternate with lovely sandy bays that face onto a transparent, turquoise sea..

144 center and bottom The Maddalena archipelago is formed by numerous tiny islets and seven large islands. Those lying further out to sea are Budelli, Razzoli and Santa Maria; those close to the mainland are Santo Stefano, Caprera, Maddalena and Spargi. The islands are connected to Gallura by sea whereas Caprera (see photograph) and Maddalena are connected by a bridge running between them.

144-145 Maddalena is the largest of the islands in the archipelago. Today it is appreciated for its natural beauty but once it was important for its strategic position. Maddalena belonged to the Pisan forces during the 13th century and became a military base under the Savoy family from the 18th century.

145 bottom left Rare strips of Corsican pines line the seashore in Iglesiente. The blues and greens separated by a strip of white rock seem to reach out to one another in vain.

145 top right Capo Coda di Cavallo (Horsetail Cape) is a promontory south of Aranci bay that points toward mainland Italy. It is an area of wild beauty with thick flora that almost reaches down to the shore and smoothly sculpted rocks that reflect in the water.

145 bottom right *Sardinia's history of continual invasions justifies the almost ever-present lookout towers around the more strategic sections of the coastline. No longer of any use, they now do no more than observe the passing of harmless pleasure boats.*

146-147 The Pink Beach on Budelli is the product of two factors: first, the abundance of coral which produces the pink sand when it is broken down, and second, the currents that concentrate the pink granules on the shore rather than take them out to sea. The natural beauty of the beach has been maintained due to the isolation of the island which has only recently been discovered by modern tourism.

148-149 The Ponte Vecchio is the oldest bridge in Florence. It has been rebuilt several times over the Arno at the point where the river is narrowest. Spared quite miraculously during World War II, it used to host the meat market; today its original appearance is derived from the small shops that line it on either side and from the passageway that passes over it built by Vasari to connect Palazzo Vecchio with Palazzo Pitti. It is one of three bridges over the Arno in Florence; the other two are the Ponte Santa Trinità and the Ponte alla Carraia.

148 bottom The Tiber in the heart of old Rome passes around the Isola Tiberina which is supposed to have assumed the shape of the boat that brought Aesculapius, the god of medicine, to Rome. Downstream there stands a single arch of the Ponte Rotto which is all that remains of a bridge rebuilt in the 16th century on the remains of the 2nd-century BC Ponte Emilio. The only ancient bridge still remaining is the Ponte Fabricio. An old hospital still stands on the Isola Tiberina, one country for a thousand cities.

One Country for a thousand cities

"Our cities are the ancient centers of all communications of a large and populous province; all roads lead to them and all local markets depend on them, they are the heart to the system of the veins; they are the destinations of consumables and the origins of industries and capital; they are a point of intersection or rather a center of gravity which cannot be assigned to any other point at random." Carlo Cattaneo's 19th century analysis of the life and purpose of cities is as true today as it was then. Italy is the country with a greater variety and richness of historical town-centers in a relatively small space than any other: large and small, ancient or simply old, on the plains or in the mountains, built on lagoons, on rivers or by the sea.

The richness of Italy's urban centers, which includes diversity and quality of architecture and monuments, is a result of their history. The mainland has only been united during the Roman Empire (up until the 5th century AD) and from 1870 to the modern day. This means that for the greater part of its history it has been separated in different states. The quality of a "state" brings in its train the development of an autonomous society, its own political, military, social and economic events and therefore also artistic and architectural achievements. Each of these states had a capital with buildings representing civil, ecclesiastical and military power: the town-hall, the cathedral, the courts and offices of its guilds. During the age of the Seigniories, these states had their own courts with the richness of buildings that such a status demanded. The courts were used for government of the state and as a representation of the governing body's

power to its subjects and nearby states of which "magnificence" was a direct expression. At different periods, Turin, Genoa, Milan, Padua, Siena, Arezzo, Mantua, Venice, Ravenna, Parma, Modena, Lucca, Florence, Rome, Naples and Palermo have all been capitals, depending on the cycle of historical events. Their urban layout and architecture are direct evidence of their moments of splendor and consequent decadence.

149 top Milan Duomo Cathedral seen from above is a majestic sight. Construction was started in 1386 by Gian Galeazzo Visconti but dragged on for the whole of the 15th and 16th centuries.

149 bottom The river Arno passes through the length of Pisa. The streets on either side of the river, here pictured from the Clock Tower, are lined with sober and discreet buildings that are lit up on every balcony on the day of the city's patron saint, St. Rainier.

150 top The Temple of Neptune and the Basilica of Paestum in Campania are located in one of the most interesting archeological sites of Italy. The Temple of Neptune was built in the mid-5th century BC in pure Doric style; the trabeation and the pediments are almost completely intact and the interior is divided into three naves. The Basilica stands on the Via Sacra and was originally dedicated to Hera (Juno); it dates from the middle of the 6th century BC and contains a peristyle of 50 Doric columns.

150 center The Temple of Segesta was built by the Dorians in 430 BC. Like the Theater it is well-preserved. It stands alone in a wide open landscape surrounded by a deep valley. It is bounded by a peristyle of 36 columns in gold-tinged limestone.

150 bottom The Temple of Concordia, in the Valley of the Temples in Agrigento, was built between 450-440 BC. It is the most impressive and majestic Doric temple in Sicily.

The history of town settlements in Italy began with the Etruscans, a people of uncertain provenance. During the 10th century BC they occupied what is now Tuscany. They then moved north of the Apennines toward Rimini, in one direction, and Mantua, in another. To the south they reached the river Sele in Campania where they founded the towns of Capua and Nola. The Latin historian Varrone noted that their town streets were based on a north-south and eastwest grid pattern. They were composed of three parts: the first one, called *arce*, which stood apart on a hill where it was used for defense and as a sanctuary; the second was the residential area and the third was the necropolis or burial ground for the dead. The necropolis is the only part to have survived intact until today. Traces of Etruscan towns still exist near Marzabotto in Emilia, at Fondi, Anagni, Segni, Ferentino, Teano and Alatri in Lazio, and at Santa Maria Capua Vetere in Campania, but they were soon replaced by Roman and medieval settlements. A strong Greek colonization started during the 8th century BC along the southern coasts and in Sicily which were included in the name *Magna Graecia.* The Greeks built ports and landing-places for their trade along the coasts of the Tyrrhenian and Ionian seas: Crotone, Locri, Sibari, Poseidonia, Naples, Cuma and, in Sicily, Naxos, Gela, Agrigento and Syracuse. Once liberated from the hold of the mother-country, these settlements became independent *polis,* city-states which transformed themselves into economic and military powers. But destruction and the sacking of these towns over the centuries have erased the cities themselves and left only the ruins of temples like at Agrigento, Paestum, Segesta and Selinunte the like of which are not found even in Greece.

150-151 The Theater of Segesta was built by the Greeks. It is in the shape of a semi-circle, 68 yards in diameter, on a rocky slope. The steps descend toward the Bay of Castellammare.

151 bottom The Island of Sardinia has many sites of great historical value: for example, the ruins of the Punic city of Tharros (left) on a panoramic rise near Oristano, and the remains of the Roman theater of Nora (right), situated near Capo di Pula.

152 left Ancient Ostia occupies a large archeological area (top) around the decumanus maximus, the main Roman road in the town. The 2nd-century BC Capitolium (center) was the largest temple in the town. The 4th-century BC house of Amore and Psyche (bottom) has preserved its mosaic floors and multicolored marbles.

152 right The ancient Roman road, Via Appia, was begun in 312 BC; today it is like an open air museum lined with the remains of villas and burial monuments from the imperial and republican eras.

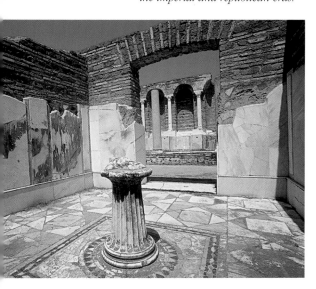

The mainland of Italy underwent new changes with the birth of the power of Rome. The Romans undertook an enormous project of territorial planning across the peninsular in which they established new cities and Romanized existing Greek and Etruscan ones. They organized a rational road system and a capillary division of the land. For the first time in history (and for the only time up until the modern era), the territory was dealt with as a whole and towns, road systems and rationalisation of the countryside were built up and developed together. Rome itself was the least typical of Roman cities because it grew in sections and was based on a unique hill situation. New Roman cities were built according to exact rules: on the flat, in a square boundary, with a grid of streets whose principal axes (called the *cardus* and *decumanus*) crossed at right angles in the center. Initially they were small

in size: Florence covered an area measuring only 20 acres originally (300 yards by 300 yards), Lucca 50 acres, Aosta 100 and Turin 130. The pre-Roman town of Pompeii was a little larger covering 186 acres and held 25,000 people. All buildings, which could reach a maximum height of 65 feet, were inserted in the grid pattern of streets. It was these, and only these, that determined the structure of the town because the lie of the land had no effect on growth. At Verona, for example, which is situated on the inside of a bend in the river

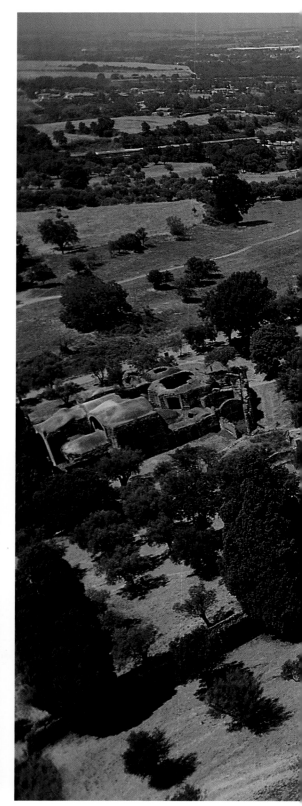

Adige, the layout of the original Roman city was not affected by the presence of the river at all. During the long period of rule, the Romans created satellite power centers like the port of Ostia, the Villa Adriana at Tivoli and towns along the Lazio coast and in Campania. Pompeii and Herculanum were the best known Roman cities and today allow us to examine Roman life directly even if their town planning was Greek and not Roman. The eruption of Vesuvius in 79 AD buried them both in a time capsule.

152-153 and 153 bottom Villa Adriana in Tivoli in the hills around Rome was built during the reign of Emperor Hadrian (AD 76-138). The villa was practically finished in 134 but Hadrian, sick and in mourning for the death of his favorite lover Antinoo, died four years later. Although the emperors that succeeded him continued to visit Tivoli, the villa was soon abandoned and fell into ruin. Between the 15th and 19th centuries, it was robbed of its art treasures which went to public and private collections. It was only since in 1870 that excavations were undertaken which brought the entire complex to light. The most impressive construction is the circular Maritime Theater (lower picture) formed by a portico and a central building separated by a canal. Moving south, the remains of a large nymphaeum can be seen and massive columns that belonged to a complex consisting of three semicircular rooms around a courtyard.

154 left The Roman town of Herculanum, traditionally founded by Hercules himself, was buried together with Pompeii by the eruption of Vesuvius in 79 AD. The city was a fishing port but also inhabited by craftsmen and a patrician class that, for its beauty and its position on the gulf of Naples, had chosen it as a place to relax in. It was divided into five districts by three principal roads (decumanus) and had a variety of house types. The torrent of mud that covered the city filled every recess, so preserving the objects made of wood, such as the roof structures, beams, stairs, doors and partitions that were burnt at Pompeii. The entire city was lost and a great part of the population that attempted to escape. Ancient frescoes and marbles works and mosaic can still be seen in the houses in Herculanum today.

In a Roman city, the forum was one of the focal points but buildings like the amphitheater or circus, used for entertainment of the people, had their own importance. These were placed on the edge of the residential area near the walls, like in Pompeii and Aosta, but sometimes outside the walls completely, like at Capua, Verona and Spoleto. Always located outside were the hippodromes (horse-racing tracks). These attracted people from around the local countryside so arrival and departure of the public was made easier. The Romans gave Italy a magnificent network of roads that reached every part of the peninsular and which today are still followed. Roads irradiated from Rome like the spokes from a wheelhub: these were the Flaminia, the Cassia, the Salaria and the Appia; a large X formed by the Postumia and the Emilia crossed the Po Valley. The countryside was "centuried," i.e., divided by a grid of small roads, each block of land measuring 767 yards (perhaps 800 paces) by 767 yards. These were assigned to veteran soldiers transformed into farmers in

times of peace. The paths are still visible in the flat countryside of Emilia, Veneto (near Padua) and Lombardy (between Cremona and Pavia). The farming soldiers of 2000 years ago determined the paths of many of today's minor roads and of the network of canals that regulates the movement of irrigation water.

154 right and 155 The city of Pompeii was founded by the Osci people in the 8th century BC but was influenced by the strong Greek colony at nearby Cuma during the 6th century BC. The town passed into the hands of the Samnites in the 5th century BC and underwent a period of prosperity until the 1st century BC. In 80 BC, Pompeii came under Roman control and became a well-known holiday town for rich Roman families who introduced new architectural and ornamental styles. At the time of the eruption of Vesuvius in AD 79, the

town had 25,000 inhabitants but within two days the town had disappeared, covered by a blanket of ash up to 22 feet deep. Systematic and official excavations only started during the 18th century under the Bourbon king, Charles III. The discovery of the town had a great effect on the public throughout Europe. The Via dell'Abbondanza (top), the red Pompeian frescoes in the Villa dei Misteri (bottom) and the large Roman Forum with the statue of Apollo (page on the right) are some of the most unusual monuments in the world.

Once the Roman empire crumbled in 476 AD, the Italian mainland was invaded by different tribes—the Lombards, Byzantines, Franks—who left clear evidence of their passing throughout the various regions, depending on the domination. In reply to these invaders, many of the old cities were abandoned by their inhabitants to live in safer locations which could be defended by walls. These new towns were often elliptical in shape with the houses built side by side to form a compact perimeter wall. There would then be one or two entrances and the town would have a tower in the center (from the 11th century on). Lucignano, Città della Pieve

and Monte San Savino are typical of this design.

New towns were built all over Italy during the Middle Ages. They were built everywhere, along rivers, on hills and on the plains based on varied designs. Often they would be adapted to fit the lie of the land meaning they might be cone-shaped, linear, stepped up the side of a hill or in a star shape. As towns increased in size and local communities became stronger, the system of using houses as a perimeter wall was no longer sufficient to defend the city so they invested in the largest and most expensive of public works and built proper town walls with towers at regular intervals. The local noble family lived in the castle which also acted as a refuge in times of war. The upper classes in some cities built houses with towers attached for personal defense: the

best example of this is at San Gimignano in Tuscany where each of the 14 towers represents the feudal origin of a noble family. In seafaring republics like Genoa and Venice, the rich merchants built the first private *palazzi*. These originally were built alongside other houses and distinguished by a particular architectural style or exterior decorations but, as they became larger, tended to occupy entire blocks.

Along the roads outside of the city walls, "suburbs" were established that were slowly integrated into the main city during subsequent expansions and surrounded by a second, exterior city wall. For the first time, buildings were constructed with porticoes which served as a covered extension for the various activities which took place on the ground floor: shops, workshops, stores etc. The porticoes in Bologna, Pavia, Treviso and

across the whole of the Po Valley were quickly copied elsewhere. Commercial buildings were the first to widen the porticoes to become galleries known as "loggias": today in Bologna there still exist the Loggia dei Mercanti (Merchants' Gallery) and the Loggia dei Banchi (Banks' Gallery) while Assisi and Terracina both have a Loggia del Grano (Wheat Gallery) and the oratory of Orsanmichele di Firenze was originally built as a commercial gallery. Each city had its own water source. A network of aqueducts was used to direct water to the public fountains which were often designed and produced by great artists or skilled craftsmen, for example, the Fontana Maggiore in Perugia, Fontana Grande in Viterbo and the Fontana Gaia, Fonte Branda and Fonte Nuova in Siena. Apart from serving a practical purpose, they also added

to the beauty of the city. Religious buildings played an important role in all towns, especially after the foundation of the two great religious orders, the Franciscans and the Dominicans. They were constructed for the first time inside the cities as opposed to the past when they were placed outside the walls. The church dedicated to the patron saint of each town had a particular importance resulting from the coupling of the building's religious offices to a function of civic representation. A town's main church might stand some distance from the cathedral but always in the center, perhaps in an elevated position, with an imposing flight of steps in front which emphasized the building's importance and its height, as for example at Siena, Todi, Arezzo, Amalfi and Salerno. Often the church was built slightly outside the residential area as in Ancona and Gubbio.

156 Construction of the austere Palazzo dei Priori in Perugia was started during the 13th century but the site was expanded over the following centuries. The façade overlooking the square includes a stately stairway up to the pulpit used for public addresses. Inside there are rooms painted with frescoes from the 16th century or lined with finely inlaid wood.

156-157 Monteriggioni is a medieval hamlet standing on a rise and enclosed by a wall. It was built in 1203 by the people of Siena as an outpost against the Florentines and passed several times from the hands of one to the other. The walls, constructed in 1213–19 and strengthened in 1260–70, are nearly 600 yards long and have 14 four-sided towers, seven of which have been rebuilt in modern times. Dante referred to the walls in a canto of his Inferno.

157 top Trento cathedral was built during the 12th-13th centuries. This majestic building in Lombard Romanesque style was placed in the center of the square where the courthouse (Palazzo Pretorio), the tower of the Town Hall (Torre Civica) and the Cazuffi-Rella houses with 15th century frescoes are situated. The city became famous for the Council of Trento held from 1545–1563 where the Church of Rome attempted to oppose Protestantism. After the Council had begun, the Counter-Reformation began bringing profound changes to Christianity.

157 center The town of Bergamo is split into two distinct sections: the lower, modern city and the upper, ancient town filled with beautiful monuments and buildings. Just behind the Colleoni Chapel stands the Contarini fountain with its imaginative sculptures.

157 bottom San Ruffino, the cathedral in Assisi, dates from the 12th century. Its Romanesque façade decorated with rose-windows is one of the most beautiful in Umbria. In this church, St. Francis, St. Clare and the emperor Frederick II were baptized.

As the power of the town or city council grew, the cities constructed town-halls for the civil government of the city which also grew in size, like the one in Siena. These *palazzi* often looked out over a large square. The squares were designed to serve the same function as the "interior" of a house and became the place where the civil, religious and commercial life of the city took place. For this reason they were built away from the main streets to be protected from traffic. Piazza del Campo in Siena is typical of this new open space. It stands against the side of a hill along the top of which runs the city's main road so that the two are completely separate. The Campo slopes downward toward the Townhall on the lower side and appears to exist for public gatherings, whether political or for entertainment, just as happens when the Palio horserace takes place twice a year. Similarly in Piazza delle Erbe in Verona or the squares in the many cities along the Via Emilia such as Forlì and Reggio Emilia. The Piazza San Petronio in Bologna is not just far away from the Via Emilia, it is also off center with regard to the network of town roads. The square is considered the center of civil, commercial and religious life (the church of the city's patron saint, St. Petronius, stands in this square while Bologna cathedral, dedicated to St. Peter, is in nearby Via Indipendenza) and illustrates a second aspect that is typical of medieval squares: the fountain of Neptune is not placed in the center. The same is found in Venice where the monument to Colleoni in Piazza SS. Giovanni e Paolo stands beside the church. No criteria for shape or size exist that are common to medieval city centers throughout Italy which means that there is no one type of square. Squares have been created throughout the country to suit the geographical conditions so that, for example, where they cover a slope, steps have been incorporated which contribute to render the surrounding monuments more imposing as with the church in Todi and the public buildings in Pistoia. Some squares exist in the shape of an "L" like in Ferrara which separates the section faced by the cathedral from that of the Town-hall. Another model is that of San Gimignano where the three squares,

"Cisterna," "del Duomo" and "delle Erbe," follow one another distinguished by the different religious or civil buildings that face onto them. Around the beginning of the 14th century, civic administrations started to embellish and improve their cities by laying out new streets, widening squares and city walls. The walls were often much longer than necessary to allow space inside for the creation of new quarters. Some cities were created from scratch for strategical purposes. Cittadella and Castelfranco Veneto were built one in front of the other to defend the Paduan and Treviso territories respectively. Pietrasanta and Camaiore were built by the administrations of Lucca to guard the boundary with Pisa; Figline Valdarno and San Giovanni Valdarno were created as outposts of the Florentine republic to defend against Arezzo. The City Council of Bologna prepared a general defense plan with the foundation of Castel San Pietro, Castelfranco Emilia and San Giorgio di Piano at the extreme southeast, northwest and northeast of the territory over which they held jurisdiction. In 1256 the town of Manfredonia was built from nothing on the orders of King Manfredi to accommodate the inhabitants of Siponto which had been destroyed by an earthquake. The layout of the cities was often in symbolic shapes. The extension and development of medieval cities throughout Italy had a profound influence on successive centuries which was not equalled until the 19th century.

158 top Piazza delle Erbe in Verona is a market-place today but it was originally a Roman forum. In the middle of the square the Market column, the 16th-century Capitello or Tribuna, the fountain of Madonna Verona topped whit St. Mark's column (1532) with a winged lion all stand in line.

158 bottom left Construction of the Franciscan church of Santa Croce was begun in 1294 and was completed in the second half of the 14th century. The façade and bell-tower, however, were erected 500 years later. The church looks onto one of the city's oldest squares.

158 bottom right The Umbrian city of Perugia has managed to retain its medieval and Renaissance appearance. The main monuments from the era of city-states center on Piazza 4 Novembre: the Palazzo dei Priori, the Fontana Maggiore and the cathedral.

159 bottom The Gothic Loggia del Lionelli in Udine is the old city hall. It takes its name from the architect who built it in 1457.

158-159 The heart of Bologna beats in piazzas Maggiore, Nettuno and Porta Ravegnana which are surrounded by the city's important buildings. Piazza Maggiore is Bologna's nerve center; besides being the result of a major medieval urban design, it has been the seat of city government and religious and cultural institutions since its inception. City hall, the palazzo of the Podestà and the church of St. Petronius all face onto it.

When the Renaissance was in full swing in the 15th century, the concept of designing the "ideal city" came into existence. It was often an intellectual exercise carried out by humanist architects on the commissions of Popes like Nicholas V, Paul III and Sixtus V, and of enlightened noblemen like Borso and Ercole d'Este and the dukes of Gonzaga. They all called in the best architects of their time to embellish, adapt and extend the capitals of their states and often, though sometimes only partially, achieved remarkable results. Perhaps the most interesting example of transformation was that of Piazza Campidoglio in Rome by Michelangelo. The artist knew how to create a masterpiece from a limited space with very different elements. He drew his idea from the obliqueness of the two existing buildings; by adding a third symmetrical building, he formed a five-sided space looking toward the palazzo in the

background.

The political and social orders underwent notable change at the end of the 16th century. Many local administrations lost their autonomy and were sucked up into a single state. Florence and Siena absorbed Pistoia, Prato, San Gimignano, Massa Marittima, Arezzo and Pisa. To the north, the whole of Veneto was ruled by the Republic of Venice which stretched as far as Brescia and Bergamo in Lombardy. Within this new political setting, a new class of merchants and bankers was formed which partly joined and partly replaced the old class of noble feudal families. To show their new power, they built expensive *palazzi* that vied for importance with public buildings, for example the Pitti Palace in Florence. The introduction of gunpowder brought a transformation to the

fortifications: towers disappeared and the walls were built thicker, lower and with the outside surface sloping to deflect cannonballs or other projectiles. The fortifications were also fitted with bastions and lunettes for more advanced techniques of defense.

During the 17th and 18th centuries, the Baroque and Neo-classical architectural styles left a firm imprint on cities throughout Italy.

The layout of the cities did not change much but the church started to adopt a more important role in the context of urban life. It became a more active religious center (this was the period of the Counter Reformation) to which cultural and social functions were added, including aid to the poor.

Large churches were built with

160 The Grand Canal and St. Mark's square are the two best known features of Venice. St. Mark's is the center and symbol of the city where the Doge and the offices of city administration and justice resided. The square is lined by the old and new offices of the Public Prosecutor and the Clock-Tower (above), and is dominated by St. Mark's church. Either side of the church stand the Sansovinian Library and the Ducal Palace (bottom).

160-161 Rome's Campidoglio square as it appears today was laid out by Michelangelo. The artist based his design around the obliqueness of the two pre-existing buildings and the creation of a third, symmetrical building to create a five sided space looking toward the palazzo in the background. To surmount the difference in level of 42 feet, he built a series of long, wide and low steps which require a slow, rhythmic pace as one mounts them. In an oval in the center of the square stands the statue of Marcus Aurelius on horseback.

convents, monasteries, hospitals or educational institutes beside them in one architectural style. The façade of the church was the focal point for an onlooker so that it became almost the wall around the square. The single family, multi-storied house from medieval times that was present throughout the Renaissance disappeared from towns.

It was replaced by rented houses that could accommodate several families.

The large and very grand noblemen's houses remained which existed almost like little courts with their servants. These buildings had large entrances to allow carriages to pass and magnificent courtyards visible from the outside. Their staircases became another opportunity for architectural fancy. Fine examples of such houses are the *palazzi* in Naples in front of the royal palace.

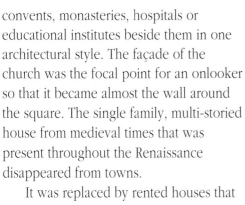

161 top Piazza del Duomo is the heart of artistic Florence. The greatest of Italian artists participated in the design of the cathedral. The dome and cupola of Santa Maria del Fiore and the bell-tower designed by Giotto dominate the Florence skyline seen from any direction.

161 center and bottom The city of Ferrara at the time of Ercole I d'Este was redesigned by Biagio Rossetti toward the end of the 15th century. The functional layout of that early version means Ferrara is today considered to have been the first real city in Europe; the two principal streets designed by Rossetti that still run through Ferrara touch on the city's main monuments: the Estense castle (center) and the cathedral (bottom) built in 1135 with its splendid and oft-restored three-part façade.

Rome and Turin were the two cities that underwent most urban transformation during the 17th and 18th centuries. Rome became Italy's true capital with constructions by the greatest artists of the time. The most significant example was the redesign of St. Peter's square, the future urban model imitated by many architects in the centuries that followed. Gianlorenzo Bernini was commissioned by Pope Alexander VII, the last pope to dedicate his energies to the renewal and enrichment of the city, to redesign the square and render it

162 top St. Peter's square is the unquestioned masterpiece of Gianlorenzo Bernini, the man who dominated artistic life in Rome in the 17th century. The colonnade that encloses the square in two long semicircles, 230 yards long in total, was constructed between 1656-67. The portico required 284 Doric columns and 88 pillars and was topped by a flat-tiled roof.

esthetical, functional and spiritual. Bernini had to include existing features, in particular the obelisk raised by Domenico Fontana on the orders of Pope Sixtus V and the fountain placed off-center by Maderno. Bernini succeeded magnificently and moreover created a square that was suited to processions and gatherings of large numbers of the faithful who crowded in to be present at blessings of the Pope from the gallery of the basilica and from the window of the papal chambers. During the 17th century, Piazza del Popolo and all the streets around it as far as Piazza Colonna also underwent transformation. On the other end, Turin tripled its size in the course of a single century. The city expanded according to a precise system of streets, Via Dora Grossa, Via Po and Via Roma, which all led into Piazza Castello so that this became the most representative part of the city center. All the large buildings along the main streets had beautiful porticoes which widened the streets to accommodate more shops and workshops.

At the beginning of the 18th century, a large construction project was undertaken in Sicily to create new or replace existing towns and villages that had been destroyed by the earthquake in 1693 in the southwest of the island. More than 50 urban centers had been ruined and 60,000 people killed. Reconstruction started immediately. Some cities, like Catania, were rebuilt on the same site but according to modern criteria; others, like Noto, Avola and Grammichele, were moved some miles away. The reconstruction of Catania was the work of architect Gian Battista Vaccarini. He designed the layout of streets and principal buildings to give the city a unified appearance. Different criteria were used in the reconstruction of Noto whose center was moved 11 miles away from the ruined town. Noto was rebuilt on the basis of the design by Angelo Italia and other local architects. The town was spread over the slopes of a hill along four parallel roads running lengthways. Three squares open onto the main road, the largest of which is the true town center. For both Avola and Grammichele, the basis of the designs was a center with radiating spokes. In the center of Avola there is a rectangular square from which four streets depart. As they continue, they widen into four other squares. In Grammichele, the central square matches the hexagonal shape of the city perimeter.

162 bottom Piazza Navona in Rome is built over Diocletian's stadium occupying its exact shape and size. In the center stands the Fountain of Rivers, a Baroque masterpiece by Bernini completed in 1651; the statues represent four rivers, symbols of the four corners of the world. The square is enclosed by palazzi and churches, one of which is Sant'Agnese in Agone by Borromini. It has a Baroque façade and a layout based on a Greek cross. The nearby 17th-century Palazzo Pamphili is especially beautiful.

162-163 Piazza San Carlo is at the center of Turin. Its square perimeter is lined with Baroque palazzi and a monument to Emanuele Filiberto stands in the center.

163 bottom left The Sicilian town of Noto was completely destroyed in 1693 but rebuilt 6 miles from its original position.

163 bottom right The elegant Sicilian port of Catania stands with Mount Etna behind. Its rectilinear streets are ornamented with Baroque monuments.

164 top The Reggia at Caserta was considered the Versailles of the kingdom of Naples. In 1752 the Bourbon king, Charles III, ordered architect Luigi Vanvitelli to construct this massive palace. Vanvitelli was the most important architect during the period of late Baroque and Neo-classical architectural styles. The grandiose, rectangular building measures 272 x 207 yards and is five floors high. Its imposing façade has 250 windows and is fronted by columns.

164 bottom and 164-165 The Reggia at Caserta is justly considered Vanvitelli's masterpiece (his original family name was Van Wittel). The Reggia is surrounded by a park designed by Luigi Vanvitelli and his son Carlo. A series of fountains and pools with statues leads from the palace to the waterfall, 256 feet high. An example of the statues is that of "Diana and Atteon" (bottom) by Vanvitelli. An English garden was created to the right of the waterfall for Maria Carolina of Austria.

Meanwhile, as the countryside became safer and more easily negotiable, large country villas belonging to noble families began to spring up, particularly in Lombardy, Veneto, Tuscany and Lazio. Whole villages would depend on these villas if they did not actually form a village in themselves. Special attention began to be paid to the inclusion of natural greenery in cities, until then largely ignored. Many parks and gardens in modern Italian cities were designed during the 18th century. In Parma and Modena, the principal aristocratic family in each ceded the gardens attached to their residences to the city council so that they could be enjoyed by the populace. In Florence several farming properties belonging to the Grand Duke just outside of the city walls were transformed into public parks; this is why some parks are known by the name "cascina" (farmhouse). In Milan, orchards and gardens belonging to monasteries and convents were confiscated to become state property for use by the public while in other cities unused military land was taken over, for example, the Lizza gardens in Siena which occupied the bulwarks and the Medici fort of Santa Barbara.

Inspired by Versailles, Charles III of Naples and Sicily commissioned Luigi Vanvitelli to design his new palace at Caserta. Progress was extremely slow, not beginning until 1753. Unfortunately, construction was not completed by 1759 when Charles abdicated to become King of Spain. He left the crown to his son Ferdinand IV who did not continue his father's project to its very end, that of making Caserta his capital.

165 bottom Vanvitelli was born in Naples in 1700. He worked in Rome, Marche and southern Italy. His greatest efforts were put into the Reggia where he attempted to combine grandeur with harmony of proportions. The interiors are also based on this same principle. The entrance hall is an example; it gives access to the courtyards, the magnificent royal staircase (to the left) and the Sala di Marte (to the right) sumptuously decorated and furnished in Imperial style.

166-167 and 167 top Villa Pisani at Stra (also called Villa Nazionale) was designed by Girolamo Frigimelica for Alvise and Almorò Pisani. Work started in 1720 and took twenty years. The rectangular design with two internal courtyards is rather severe but the park, the stables, the "casa dei freschi" on the hill, the open-air theater and the tower in the park walls are more decorative. The rooms are decorated with high quality frescoes like that by Gianbattista Tiepolo (top right photograph) entitled La Gloria.

166 bottom left The Rotonda near Vicenza is a celebrated work by Palladio. The square-based building is topped by a cupola. A colonnaded pediment opens on each side.

166 bottom right The Palladian Villa Foscari, known as the Malcontenta, stands on a bend in the river Brenta. The name comes from a Venetian noblewoman of the Foscari family who was rather displeased at being relegated from the city to this villa.
167 center Villa Giovannelli in the unmistakable style of Palladio stands at Noventa on the river Brenta.

167 bottom Villa Elmo at Montecchia was commissioned around 1568 by Gabriele Capodilista from Dario Varotari, the Venetian architect and painter. Capodilista had been awarded the estate of Montecchia and wanted to create a house worthy of a nobleman. The villa's principal feature is that it was designed by the same person that created the pictorial decorations. Consequently, the building is an example of harmony of architecture and decoration.

168 top left The traditional images of Naples (the view of the bay at the feet of the Posillipo hill or the Vomero or lanes with children playing in front of the slums) are a world away from that of the modern and tall buildings in the business area, yet these two sides of the city exist just a few hundred yards from one another. The old quarter of Porta Capuana and that of the new offices are both close to the central station.

168 bottom left The glass and steel north tower of Skidmor, Owings and Merryl, named "Matitone" by the Genoese, rises shining out of the skyline of the Ligurian capital.

During the 19th century only small towns were created but, in imitation of Napoleonic France, large urban reorganisations took place. In Milan the Foro Bonaparte was opened which, when connected with the triumphal arch at the start of Corso Sempione, was the road which led to France. For this to be realized, the area around the Castle had to be transformed. The ramparts around Castello Sforzesco were demolished (as happened in many places in Italy in the euphoria of the Napoleonic occupation) which until 1801 had been a true Renaissance citadel. The resulting material was used to build the Arena to be used for sporting events which was inaugurated in 1807 in Napoleon's presence.

Following the earthquake of 1783, the reconstruction of Messina took place. The reconstruction of the palace overlooking the sea was based on the design by Minutolo and included a Neo-classical arcade formed by colossal semi-columns. The entire construction was the pride of the town's inhabitants until 1908 when the next earthquake destroyed the new palace completely.

The Industrial Revolution reached Italy from England and had a profound effect on the cities, especially those in the north where factories and new houses sprang up to accommodate the workers. In the 20th century, the Fascists drained many of the marshes in Lazio where they founded a number of new cities, many of which were designed by Marcello Piacentini, to populate those areas; for example, Sabaudia, Latina and Aprilia. Other towns were created in Sardinia for agricultural and mining purposes, all of which reflected the rationalist urban concepts of the 1920s and 30s.

At the end of World War II, Italy had lost 5% of its housing and suffered huge damage to its artistic heritage. Reconstruction was not organized and suffered accordingly; city centers were assaulted by speculators and suburbs were thrown up in a disorganized manner to create dormitory areas. When the economic boom came in the 1960s, the history of Italian cities coincided with that of the new tourist resorts at the seaside, by the lakes

and in the mountains. Nearly all of these were created without thought to the character that had permeated Italian city planning for centuries. Today, for better or worse, Italian cities reflect those two thousand years of life. They are "natural centers," according to the definition of Carlo Cattaneo, from which man "cannot easily separate," because "they are the work of centuries and of remotest events ... whose causes are older than memory." The history of Italian cities is in fact the history of the Italians.

168 top right The Foro Bonaparte was designed in 1802 by town planner Giovanni Antolini in honor of Napoleon and should have surrounded all of Castello Sforzesco but the project which also included the Arena and the Arco was never finished.

168 bottom right Milan has undergone more development in this century than any other city. During the years of the economic boom, the Pirelli skyscraper, inaugurated in 1959, became a new symbol of the city.

169 Milan's Castello Sforzesco has experienced many episodes of construction, destruction, development and restoration in its centuries of history. The version seen today is the reconstruction undertaken at the end of the 19th century by architect Luca Beltrami.

170 top Piazza del Popolo is an oval closed by the twin churches of Santa Maria di Montesanto and Santa Maria dei Miracoli and by the Pincio gardens the square is a meeting place for Romans. The Flaminio obelisk stands in the center.

170 center The Vittoriale is the monument erected to king Vittorio Emanuele II of Italy at the turn of the 20th century. It stands in Piazza Venezia in Rome. The tomb of the Unknown Soldier rests inside.

170 bottom Trinità dei Monti is the name that combines a square, a flight of steps and a church. With Piazza di Spagna and the elegant Via Condotti below, the area is one of the most "recherché" corners of Rome.

ROME:

THE ETERNAL CITY

170-171 Tradition has it that the Eternal City, Rome, was first settled here, on Palatine Hill and in the area occupied by the Forum, between the end of the 9th and start of the 7th century BC.

171 top left The Tomb of Augustus is a circular construction 98 yards in diameter on which work was begun in 27 BC. Once it lost its original function as an imperial tomb, it was transformed into a pit for building materials, a hanging garden, an amphitheater and an auditorium.

171 top right Construction of the Baths of Caracalla began in AD 212. The baths remained operative until the invasion of the Goths in 537. At the center of the baths is a large section measuring 240 x 125 yards surrounded by fenced grassy areas.

172-173 In AD 69, Vespasian started construction of the Flavius Amphitheater, one of Rome's most famous symbols, known as the Colosseum. The outermost of the four rings that comprised it supported the wooden beam the velarium was fixed to, the large cloth that protected people from rain and sun.

174 center left Construction of the Pantheon was started in 27 AD as a place of worship, first for the gods of the republican and imperial Romans, later for Christians; but despite continuous alterations it has survived until the modern day. It is based on the layout of the ancient thòlos, a circular building typical of Aegean civilisation. The dome of the Pantheon is 141 feet across, exactly the distance of its height from the ground, which gives it a spherical and harmonious proportion emphasized by the light that enters from the hole in the top. The outer colonnade has disappeared from the original construction and a grander entrance has been "invented" in its place.

174 bottom left Next to Trajan's Forum stand the Trajan Markets, separated from the Palatine Hill by the road, the Via dei Fori Imperiali. The markets were a large commercial area in the 2nd century AD which housed more than 150 shops and offices.

174 right The statue of the Prima Porta is the most famous of the more than 80 erected in honor of Octavian Augustus, one of the founders of imperial Rome.

174-175 The Temple of Castor and Pollux was named for the twin sons of the god Jove. Its alternative name is the Temple of the Dioscuris and is one of Rome's most ancient monuments. It was originally constructed in 484 BC but subsequently rebuilt several times.

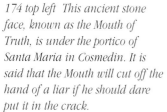

174 top left This ancient stone face, known as the Mouth of Truth, is under the portico of Santa Maria in Cosmedin. It is said that the Mouth will cut off the hand of a liar if he should dare put it in the crack.

175 bottom left Constantine's Arch was inaugurated in AD 315 to celebrate the victory of Constantine over Massenzius. It has splendid bas-reliefs taken from previous monuments. The arch stands in the Colosseum square.

175 bottom right The road that passes through the Forum area and runs as far as the Colosseum, the Via dei Fori Imperiali, was built by the Fascists as a stage for military parades.

PIVS·VII·PONT·MAX·
QVOD·ABSOLVENDVM·SVPERERAT
ADDITO·CRATERE·EXCITATO·SALIENTE
SYMPLEGMA·CONSVMMAVIT
A·D·MDCCCXVIII·PONTIF·XIX·

176-177 The Quirinale is the seat of the President of the Republic of Italy and takes its name from the hill it was built on. The façade is a typical late Renaissance design by the architect Fontana.

176 bottom The so-called "chick" is in fact a baby elephant that supports the small Egyptian obelisk in Piazza della Minerva. Splendid Baroque palazzi provide a wonderful backdrop to the unusual monument.

177 top right Marcus Aurelius' column has a spiral frieze that recounts the military victories of the emperor. It stands in Piazza Colonna and is surrounded by Palazzo Ferraioli, Palazzo Colonna and Palazzo Chigi, seat of the Prime Minister.

177 bottom right The imposing pyramid of Caius Cestius is joined to the Aurelian wall. Built in the Egyptian style, which was fashionable after the conquests there, it is 118 high and has a base width of 98 feet per side. It was built as a tomb for the praetor, Caius Cestius Epulone.

177 top left Isola Tiberina, the island in the river Tiber, has been home to a hospital since ancient times and is also land that has been consecrated to Aesculapius, god of medicine. Roman tradition tells that the island was inhabited by the snake sacred to Aesculapius; after Aesculapius fell out of the boat bringing him to Rome, the Romans shaped the island like a boat.

177 bottom left The Barcaccia is the name given to the fountain in the center of Piazza di Spagna. It was commissioned by Pope Urban VIII Barberini in 1629 from Pietro Bernini, father of Gianlorenzo Bernini. It is in the shape of a boat that seems to float in a tank placed lower than the level of the square.

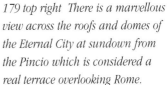

179 top right There is a marvellous view across the roofs and domes of the Eternal City at sundown from the Pincio which is considered a real terrace overlooking Rome.

179 bottom right Via Sistina is the road that connects Piazza Barberini with Trinità dei Monti. The Sistine Theater and Baroque church of SS. Ildefonso and Tommaso da Villanova.

180-181 All Rome's greatest artists during the first half of the 1700's worked on the Trevi Fountain. The magnificent work covers the whole of one side of Palazzo Poli.

178 top left The Fontana dei Fiumi (Fountain of Rivers) in Piazza Navona is one of Gianlorenzo Bernini's masterpieces. Built in 1651, the fountain represents the personifications of the rivers Ganges, Danube, Plate and (shown in the picture) Nile. The head of the Nile is veiled because at that time its source was still unknown.

178 top right Campo de' Fiori today hosts the fruit and vegetable market but at one time it was a site for games, races and even executions. The most famous person to die there was the philosopher Giordano Bruno who was burnt alive in 1600 after an eight years long trial. A statue to him stands in the center of the square.

178-179 The Spanish Steps join Piazza di Spagna with the church of Trinità dei Monti. It is a favorite setting for fashion shows and a meeting place for Romans and tourists.

179 left The shape of Piazza Navona recalls the shape of Diocletian's sports stadium over which it was built. The name Navona is thought to have derived from the ancient word agoni meaning struggle (i.e. the sporting competition); this probably developed into n'agone (therefore nagone) and then to the actual Navona.

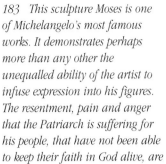

183 This sculpture Moses is one of Michelangelo's most famous works. It demonstrates perhaps more than any other the unequalled ability of the artist to infuse expression into his figures. The resentment, pain and anger that the Patriarch is suffering for his people, that have not been able to keep their faith in God alive, are shown in Moses' face, the solemnity of his figure and the vibrant tension of his muscles. The masterpiece stands in the mausoleum of Pope Julius II in the church of San Pietro in Vincoli. The mausoleum was designed by Michelangelo over a period of 40 years, with various interruptions, starting in 1513.

182 top left The Passion of Christ is represented along the Sant'Angelo bridge, which leads to the castle of the same name. The statues of the angels that hold up the symbols of the Passion were designed by Bernini but sculpted by his pupils.

182 bottom left Castel Sant'Angelo is one of the capital's most famous monuments. Erected between AD 130 and 140 as the tomb for Hadrian, it was turned into a fortress, then a prison and then as papa residence. The massive cylindrical building today is enclosed inside a square wall and houses the National Museum of Castel Sant'Angelo.

182 top right The solemn interior of the Basilica of San Giovanni in Laterano has a layout in the form of a Latin cross and five naves. Its current appearance was the work of Borromini who was commissioned by Pope Clement XI to restore it for the Jubilee of 1650.

182 bottom right The church of St. Mary in Trastevere has very ancient origins and is built in the square of the same name; it was the first church in Rome to be dedicated to the cult of the Virgin. The beautiful façade is decorated with mosaics from the 12th-13th centuries which depict Mary seated on a throne surrounded by ten saints.

184-185 *The construction of Via della Conciliazione was a work of great symbolic value but is debatable from a town-planning point of view. Built between 1936–50, it required the demolition of old district of Santo Spirito and Sant'Angelo. The road stretches from the river Tiber to St. Peter's Square.*

184 bottom left *St. Peter's Square is Bernini's masterpiece. Created in 1656, it is made up of two semi-circles formed by four rows of Doric columns, that ring the entire area in front of the church, and by 140 statues of saints. For many, this is the true heart of Christianity, the area where the words of the Pope can be heard.*

184 bottom right *The Swiss Guard has been the armed force of the Vatican for over 500 years. The corps consists of 100 men whose purpose is to protect the life of the Pope.*

185 bottom left *Five bronze doors give access to the interior of St. Peter's. The canopy over the papal altar, designed by Bernini, stands in the majestic Baroque nave directly below Michelangelo's dome.*

185 top right *The church of St. Peter dominates the aerial view of the city: it covers 5.5 acres, is 239 yards long, 125 yards wide at the façade and the basic structure is 154 feet high.*

185 bottom right *The dome over St. Peter's was designed by Michelangelo. The vault is divided into 16 segments and is in two layers. The dome is 139 feet in diameter and has a total height of 449 feet.*

186 The Pietà was executed by
Michelangelo in 1499 when he was
hardly twenty five years old but
already at the height of his powers.
It is the only work to bear the
signature of the reserved and
unconventional artist.
For its capacity to convey the
abandonment of the dead Christ
and the silent but dignified pain of
the Virgin and for the softness of

the Virgin's drapery which hardly
seems sculpted from marble but
modelled in clay, the Pietà has
been praised by many as the sum
total of the extraordinary talents
of Michelangelo. Perhaps because
the statue has such great artistic
and symbolic value, it has been
subject to acts of vandalism in the
past. The masterpiece is housed in
Saint Peter's in Rome.

187 In Greek mythology, Laocoön,
the son of Priam, was a priest of
Apollo. When he tried to dissuade
the Trojans from bringing the
wooden horse into the city, he and
his two sons were strangled by two
sea serpents sent by Athena. The
episode inspired several classical
sculptors, for example, Agesandro,
Polidoro and Atanadoro from the
island of Rhodes who, according to

historians and critics, seem to have
been the creators of the group
portrayed and now kept in the
Vatican Museum. The work is so
amazingly plastic that was praised as
a masterpiece by Pliny and was
chosen as an ornament for the
palace of the emperor Titus. The work
is probably an original from
Pergamum and imported to Rome
during the 2nd century BC.

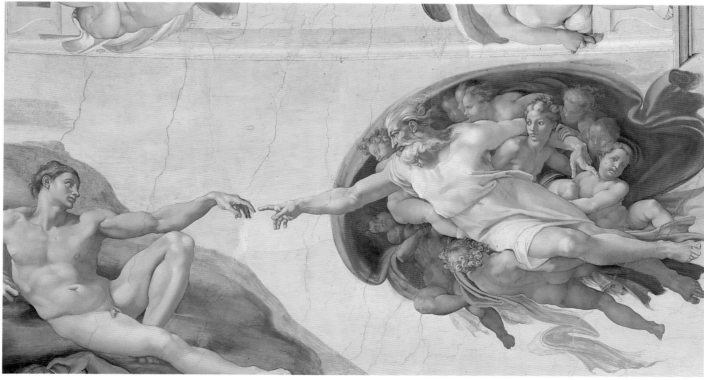

188-189 The Sistine Chapel takes its name from Pope Sixtus IV who had it built between 1475-81. The rectangular chapel measures 131 x 46 feet and is 69 feet high. The walls and barrel vaults are decorated with frescoes by Botticelli, Ghirlandaio, Pinturicchio and Signorelli but what has made the chapel a masterpiece known all over the world is the work by Michelangelo who was commissioned by Pope Julius II to add to the work. The artist worked on the ceiling (see photograph) from 1508-12 and on the wall behind the altar (The Last Judgement over 2100 square feet) which he finished in 1541.

188 and 189 bottom The theme of the Sistine Chapel ceiling is taken from the Book of Genesis. Michelangelo divided the central part of the ceiling in nine scenes and surrounded them with decorative motifs and trompe l'oeil with the so-called ignudi that support the false stuccowork in order to give depth to the massive fresco. Around the nine episodes taken from the Book of Genesis, Michelangelo positioned seven gigantic prophets and five sybils. The nine incidents portrayed are (from the great altar): The Separation of Light and Darkness, The Creation of the Stars, The Separation of Water and Earth, The Creation of Adam (left), The Creation of Eve, The Original Sin and Banishment from Paradise (right), The Sacrifice of Noah, The Flood and Noah's Drunkenness.

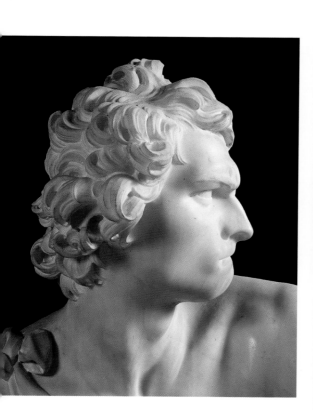

190 bottom left and right David firing his sling by Gianlorenzo Bernini in 1623 is one of the many sculptures on show in the Borghese Gallery. The face of David is said to be a self-portrait. Bernini was the first to use a spiral movement to give the illusion of vitality to a sculpture, a technique he used on many occasions. Bernini's artistic qualities, like those of many geniuse's of his era, were demonstrated in numerous fields: he was later to prove himself a brilliant architect and engineer, as shown by the colonnade at St. Peter's and the fountains in Piazza Navona.

190 top left and 191 One of Antonio Canova's most well-known masterpieces, Paolina Borghese, sculpted between 1805-08, is now kept in the Borghese Gallery. The portrait of the aristocratic Roman reclining in an attitude reminiscent of Venus is one of the sculptor's most artistically successful works. Like other works in marble, it was expressly commissioned from the Venetian artist by the rich Borghese family.

192-193 Apollo and Daphne is a sculpture by Bernini from 1624, also to be seen in the Borghese Gallery. It is the most famous work of the artist as a young man. He was born in Naples but moved to Rome to oblige his patron, Pope Paul V Borghese, following which Bernini became the official portraitist of the patrician Borghese family.

194-195 *The Raphael rooms are a series of unquestioned masterpieces in the Vatican Museums. The rooms were already sumptuous in 1505 when Pope Julius II engaged Raphael to enrich them further. Raphael and the members of his school worked on the four rectangular rooms with cross vaults from 1508-17. The last of the rooms to be completed is shown in the picture and takes its name from the fresco The Burning of the Town.*

195 top Also the Loggias of Raphael were completed by his pupils using the designs and sketches of the Master. The vaults show episodes from the Old Testament and the life of Jesus.

195 bottom The Eliodorus Room also takes its name from one of the frescoes painted by Raphael himself: The Expulsion of Eliodorus from the Temple. The cycle of works in this room were prepared by Pope Julius II himself.

194 bottom Constantine Room is one of the famous Raphael rooms and was used for official receptions in the Vatican. It is decorated with frescoes showing important episodes in the life of the Emperor Constantine—his Baptism, The Battle of Ponte Milvio, The Apparition of the Cross and The Donation of Rome which were designed by Raphael but completed after his death by his pupils. Raphael Sanzio, born in Urbino, died in Rome in 1520 aged only 37 years old.

197 top The relationship of Turin with the Alps is very close. Ever since it was a Roman city called Augusta Taurinorum, the city has been an important stopping-off point on the way to Gaul from the rest of Italy.

197 center Palazzo Carignano is a magnificent example of the best of Turin Baroque architecture. It dates from the 17th century and is linked with important historical episodes: it was here that the Kingdom of Italy was proclaimed and here that its first Parliament met.

197 bottom The foliage of the trees embraces Corso Vittorio Emanuele II, one of the main streets that cross Turin east-west.

TURIN:
THE "LITTLE OLD LADY'S" DRAWING ROOM

196 top left Seen from the Gran Madre, over Vittorio Emanuele I bridge, Piazza Vittorio Veneto is a square bordered by Piedmontese Baroque buildings that seems to give access to the heart of the city and, more distantly, the Alps.

196 top right Porta Palatina, a section of the old Turin walls still in a good state of repair, dates from the 1st century AD. In the square dominated by the two crenellated towers, the statues of Julius Caesar and Octavian, two copies of the originals still look over what remains of the Roman road.

196-197 At the foot of the Alps, Turin preserves obvious traces of what was the capital of Savoyard Italy: the elegance of the palazzi in the old center, the geometrical design of its street layout and the large and well looked after parks. The grandiose 18th-century Mole Antonelliana, symbol of the city, overlooks the city skyline from 551 feet of hight.

198-199 The river Po crosses the city north-south passing through the center where Valentino Park and Piazza Vittorio Veneto are to be found. In this section (photograph of the Murazzi), the severe, elegant Piedmont-style palazzi are reflected in the waters, not always clean, of the river.

198 bottom Turin's most beautiful and inaccessible villas stand on the hill east of the Gran Madre and the Valentino in large natural settings. This is the most exclusive area of the city, sought after by those who wish to escape the confusion and traffic of the city center.

199 top The Gran Madre (left) and Mount Capuccini, with the church of Santa Maria del Monte and the Capucin monastery (right) face the Po near Vittorio Emanuele I bridge. This hill rises to the villages of Pino Torinese and Pecetto from the river. It is the greenest area of Turin and dotted with large, expensive houses. The National Museum of the Mountains Duca degli Abruzzi is also situated here.

199 center Valentino Castle is a strong and severe fortification on the bank of the Po, built in 1630 by Carlo di Castellamonte who took 16th-century French castles as his model. The fortress is surrounded by the 130-acre Valentino Park, created in 1830 by the Savoy family on the east bank of the river.

199 bottom The Borgo and the Medieval Castle are an unusual set of buildings built in Valentino Park last century to reproduce medieval constructions of Piedmont and the Aosta valley on behalf of the Savoy family.

200 Palazzo Madama stands in Piazza Castello, the heart of Turin. The body of the building is medieval and is built around the remains of a Roman doorway. The castle was used as a residence from 15th-17th centuries by the royal Savoy family. It was heavily remodelled in the 18th century with the creation of the present imposing façade photograph) designed by Filippo Juvarra, the great Spanish architect. Now the building is used to house the Civic Museum of Ancient Art.

201 top left San Lorenzo is the Baroque masterpiece of Guarino Guarini. Born in Modena in 1624, the architect learned his trade by studying the buildings of Borromini, then developed his own style of highly imaginative geometrical forms. San Lorenzo is the epitome of this style: inside, its central body features extensive stuccowork and the use of marble and gold-leaf decoration, the outside is gentle and harmonious with an attractive cupola (see photograph).

201 center left Palazzo Reale was built in 1660 in the sober and elegant style it still displays. It faces onto Piazza Reale, an extension of Piazza Castello, while its lovely park behind has been turned into public gardens. Until 1865, the palazzo was a Savoyard residence; now, its right wing houses one of the best collections of arms in Europe for pieces made between the 16th and 19th centuries.

201 bottom left The spirit of the Baroque style pervades the sumptuous and elegant interior of Palazzo Reale. The Throne Room where the king held audience was for years the center of Savoyard power. The regalness of the room is evident in the quality of the decorations: the inlaid wooden floors, the gilded stuccowork, the enormous chandeliers and the purple velvet drapes that cover the canopy.

201 right The reception rooms on the first floor of Palazzo Reale are open to the public. They are decorated in the styles of 17th-19th centuries with magnificent tapestries, furniture and other furnishings of superb manufacture. Unfortunately, part of this splendid building was destroyed by a fire in 1997 but the damage is being repaired and restoration is being carried out in the minutest detail.

202 top left Piazza Ducale is the pride of Vigevano, an industrial town in the province of Pavia. The cathedral that faces onto it is 1000 years old but has a 17th-century façade.

202 top right Ivrea was originally a Roman town and a Savoyard fiefdom along the Dora Baltea and ancient Via Francigeno. Evidence of its importance in the past are the 10th-century cathedral and 13th-century castle.

AMONG RICE FIELDS AND ANCIENT CHARTERHOUSES

202-203 The Certosa (Charterhouse) was built on the wishes of Gian Galeazzo Visconti. It stands 5 miles from Pavia and was started in 1396. The complex includes a large and a small cloister. Inside there are paintings by Borgognone and his school, Perugino, Guercino, Morazzone, Macrino d'Alba and Luini. The transept of the church includes funeral monuments of Beatrice d'Este and Ludovico il Moro.

203 top The church of St. Andrew, built in 1219 in Vercelli, is one of Italy's best examples of Cistercian Gothic architecture. Two towers stand on either side of the church façade; the lunette illustrating The Martyrdom of St. Andrew by Antelami, is a masterpiece. Inside, the three naves have ogival vaults.

203 bottom The symbol of Novara is the church of St. Gaudenzio with its large dome, nearly 400 feet high. It was designed by the architect Antonelli who also designed the Mole in Turin. The church is from the 16th century but the dome was added in 1888.

204 top The Arch of Peace stands at the beginning of the road that leads to Sempione Park. Topped by a bronze chariot, it was designed by Luigi Cagnola in celebration of the triumph of Napoleon.

204 bottom The Madonnina is a 17 foot high statue that stands on top of Milan Cathedral at a height of 350 feet. It is made of copper and coated with 300 grammes of gold. It was placed on the highest pinnacle of the cathedral in 1774 when Milan was controlled by the Austrians. The original version, by Giuseppe Peregò, was made from wood and is kept in the Cathedral Museum.

MILAN:
THE CITY THAT NEVER SLEEPS

204-205 The cathedral is without doubt the building that symbolizes the city. It is decorated with 3159 statues and even more pinnacles, the highest of which is 354 feet high and supports the Madonnina. Gian Galeazzo Visconti encouraged construction of the cathedral which began in 1386 but its majestic façade was only completed in the 19th century by the architects, Amati and Zanoia.

205 top left The tall buildings and towers that rise up behind the cathedral testify to the close relationship between historical and artistic Milan and the world of business. In the distance, though not so close to the city, stand the Alps.

205 top right The 19th-century façade of the cathedral is lit up with a warm glow toward the end of a winter's afternoon. In the foreground, in the center of the square, stands the monument to Vittorio Emanuele II.

206 top left The Guastalla gardens, Sempione Park and the area around the Sforzesco castle are the only open areas of the polluted and traffic-ridden city which, however, is required to provide quality of life for its inhabitants.

206 bottom left Villa Comunale faces onto Via Palestro. It was built in Neo-classical style by the Viennese architect Leopold Pollack, pupil of Piermarini. Pollack was very active professionally in Lombardy at the end of the 18th and start of the 19th centuries. Villa Comunale, also known as Palazzo Belgioioso, was partially damaged by a terrorist's bomb in 1993; nowadays it is home to the Gallery of Modern Art.

206 top right Via Dante is one of Milan's main streets and connects two of the most important areas of the city: Piazza Cordusio and Castello Sforzesco (seen in the distance). The street is home to the Piccolo Teatro.

206 bottom right and 207 bottom left Milan is a middle-class city but filled with beautiful houses and elegant private courtyards enclosing hidden gardens. Typical treasures concealed in old Milan, they hide a few columns, a portico, an Art Nouveau gate and ivy climbing over the plasterwork.

206-207 The statue of Giuseppe Garibaldi on horseback surveys Largo Cairoli and its incessant traffic. In the distance stands Castello Sforzesco built in 1450 over the 14th-century Visconti fort. Actually, the only remains of the Visconti building are to be seen in the elegant features of the tower. The crenellated walls and large towers built by the Spaniards in the 16th–17th centuries are a reminder that the castle was practically impregnable for centuries.

207 bottom right The Grande Disco by Arnaldo Pomodoro stands in Piazza Meda. It is one of the many works of art around the city, capital of modern culture and center of everything innovative in Italy.

208 top right The Galleria Vittorio Emanuele II was designed by Giuseppe Mengari between 1865-77. It is an elegant, 18th-century drawing-room that connects Piazza Duomo to Piazza della Scala. It is loved by both the Milanese and tourists and is a favorite place for a stroll, particularly in winter when the glass roof ensures shelter from the cold, misty air of the Po valley.

208 center The Galleria Vittorio Emanuele II, which is 218 yards long on its longer side, is shaped like a cross. In the center where the two arms meet, the floor is decorated with an enormous rose in colored inlaid marble. Every aspect of the Galleria is typical of 19th-century style: the architect, Mengoni, wanted it to be elegant and solemn, in keeping with its role as the lively center of the city.

208 bottom left There cannot be a music enthusiast in the world who does not want to visit La Scala. The theater's name comes from that of an old church, Santa Maria alla Scala, which was built by Regina della Scala, wife of Bernabò Visconti. The church fell down in 1776 and the theater, with its luxurious interior and perfect acoustics, was raised from its ruins, following a project by Piermarini.

208-209 The octagon where the two walkways of the Galleria Vittorio Emanuele intersect is illuminated by the light from the enormous glass dome above. Several of Milan's most famous and elegant restaurants and bars are to be found under the glass roof of the Galleria, where the heart of Milan beats most strongly.

209 top left Milan's most beautiful luxury shops are located in an area bounded by Via Montenapoleone, Via della Spiga, Via Sant'Andrea and Via Santo Spirito. Here the visitor will find the shops of Armani, Ferré, Versace, Prado, Gucci, Krizia, Valentino and Trussadi, arbiters of fashion around the world.

209 top right Milan has made fashion into a huge industry and has always been the "city of tailors." It does not have a tradition of great aristocrats or noble families, rather, it is the city of workers which will happily reward successful entrepreneurs, artists, editors or stylists, whoever they may be.

210 top Santa Maria delle Grazie was built in the mid-15th century in a Lombard-Gothic style by architect Guiniforte Solari. During his career, spent mostly in Lombardy, Solari was also responsible for the construction of the interior of the Certosa of Pavia. The lantern on the church roof and the Renaissance platform inside were later modified by Bramante.

210 bottom From Piazza della Vetra, the perimeter, early Christian towers and the drum and cupola rebuilt at the end of the 16th century of the church of San Lorenzo Maggiore can be clearly seen. On the front side of the church some of the most impressive remains from ancient Milan have been preserved: several Attic-Corinthian columns rebuilt to form a four-sided portico and the statue of Emperor Constantine.

211 The Basilica of St. Ambrose and the Duomo are Milan's two most important churches. St. Ambrose's church was originally built in 386 during the life of Ambrose himself (patron saint of Milan). From the 7th-9th centuries it was altered several times until it took on its present form, that of a solid and beautiful Romanesque church.

212-213 Andrea Mantegna was born in Padua but trained in the Tuscan school of painters. He was a pupil of Donatello and Piero della Francesca. They taught him the rules of perspective which he fused with the study of colors typical of the Venetian school from which he came. His Cristo in Scurto from the end of the 15th century seems a happy combination of both schools. Compared to the frescoes Mantegna painted in the Ducal Palace in Mantua, here we see an intention to disturb through the subtle play of expressions and the use of harsh, gloomy light.

213 The Marriage of the Virgin by Raphael in 1504 is displayed in the Pinacoteca di Brera. Besides being one the painter's masterpieces, it also has strong symbolic and historical values: experts have recognized clear references to Tuscan and Roman settings, where Raphael worked at the start of the 16th century, in the figures and background scenery. For example, to terminate the perspective, Raphael has painted a round temple just like Bramante's San Pietro in Montorio built two years before in Rome.

214 center and bottom left
Fairs, local festivals and antique markets are some of the occasions on which the Navigli become the center of Milanese life again. This quarter of the city is called Porta Ticinese; it grew up around the dockyard and is filled with lanes and tiny shops.

214 top left and right After the Cerchia ring canal was covered, the Navigli canals lost the role they had played for centuries. At the end of the 20th century, what remains of the Navigli is making a comeback. The Darsena, Naviglio Grande and Naviglio Pavese canals have their origin at Piazza 24th May, traditionally a site of markets and gatherings. At one time this area was the haunt *of low life but today has become a center of night life: pubs, music bars, restaurants etc. The inhabitants of the large blocks of flats have accepted that the new influx is the price they have to pay for bringing this area back to life. The old inns and shops have been restored and reopened and the slow waters of the Navigli have begun to reflect Milanese life once more.*

215 Milan is also a city of water and has made use of deviated water courses since classical times. Originally they were used as a means of defense: an ancient dyke fed by the Seveso, Nirone and Mussa streams ringed the Roman walls but now is part of a drainage system. A second dyke, dug and fortified in 1156 and called the Inner Dyke, corresponded to what today is called the "Cerchia dei Navigli." In fact, the Cerchia was almost completely covered for reasons of *hygiene and "decorum" in the 1930s. The first navigable canal was the Naviglio Grande which was dug to facilitate transport of materials for construction of the cathedral. The special flat-bottomed boats carried marble and lumber for centuries. The Naviglio della Martesana, which terminated at Brera, was dug in 1457. The Naviglio Pavese which connects Milan to Pavia was the last to be completed, whereas the Naviglio Paderno was designed by Leonardo da Vinci.*

216 left Dedicated to St. Alexander, Bergamo cathedral was first built during the Longobard era but rebuilt several times from the 13th-17th centuries. The cathedral is laid out on the plan of a Latin cross with a single large nave. Inside there are paintings by Tiepolo, Previtali and Moroni. The greenish dome of the cathedral and the dome of the Colleoni Chapel are the two symbols of the upper city; Piazza Duomo, in the center, is surrounded by Bergamo's most important monuments.

216 top right Seen from a hill above upper Bergamo, the Lombard city looks like a succession of houses and hills. At the top left of the picture, the domes of the cathedral and the Colleoni Chapel and the Torre del Gombito can be seen. Ancient Bergamo (the upper city) is completely walled; the lower, modern city is the result of the industrial boom the city has enjoyed since World War II.

BERGAMO AND BRESCIA:
CLASSICAL PASTS, MODERN PRESENTS

216 bottom right Piazza della Loggia is the "drawing room" onto which Brescia's most famous buildings face: the Monte di Pietà (15th century) and the Clocktower. The square was the scene of a terrorist bomb in 1974 whose victims are remembered by a memorial stone. The square is named after the Loggia, the City Hall, which was built between the end of the 15th and mid-16th centuries.

217 Built between 1472-76 as a monument to the famous troop commander, Bartolomeo Colleoni, the Coileoni Chapel is probably Bergamo's most important building. Built in typical Renaissance style in the upper city by architect Giovanni Antonio Amadeo, the Chapel has a dynamic façade with colored marble, fretwork and rich ornamentation. Inside, frescoes by Tiepolo decorate the wall lunettes.

219 top The picture shows a detail of the face on the Clocktower in Piazza delle Erbe built in 1473 by Luca Fancelli.

219 center Palazzo Te was built on a single-storey, square design in 1525 by Giulio Romano for Federico II Gonzaga. Today it houses the Palazzo Te Civic Museum. The unusual name comes from the locality in which the palazzo was built: Teijto, later shortened as "Te."

MANTUA:

THE CITY OF THE GONZAGA FAMILY

218 top left The old city center of Mantua is seen here from the so-called "Smaller Lake" created by a bend in the river Mincio as it passes around the city. The cathedral and St. George's castle are recognisable among the ancient palazzi.

218 top right The medieval buildings that line Piazza delle Erbe include the 13th-century Palazzo della Ragione, the 14th-century Clocktower, the Renaissance Rotonda di San Lorenzo and the church of St. Andrew.

218-219 and 219 bottom The Sala dei Giganti in the Palazzo Te was decorated by Giuliano Romano and his school in the first half of the 16th century. The vault fresco Olympus depicts Jove's revenge on the rebel giants.

220 top The National Museum of Ravenna is housed in the cloisters of the ancient monastery of St. Vitale. It holds an interesting collection of Roman, early Christian, Gothic and Byzantine pieces. The early Christian church of St. Vitale dates from the 6th century; the interior of the octagonal body of the building is decorated with a mosaic cycle in Byzantine style from the 6th century.

220 center The church of St. Apollinaire in Classe stands three miles from Ravenna where its port, Classe, once existed. It was built with three naves and a wide atrium (now lost) by Giuliano Argentario in the 6th century. The huge cylindrical bell-tower was built at a later date.

RAVENNA:
A BYZANTINE ATMOSPHERE

220 bottom Important Byzantine sarcophagi stand along the side naves of St. Apollinaire in Classe, separated from the central nave by elegant marble columns. Splendid 6th and 7th century mosaics decorate the apsidal bowl-shaped vault and the triumphal arch.

220-221 The treasures of the monastery of St. Vitale are the fretwork of the capitals, the marble and, above all, the mosaic cycle which shows emperors, bishops and their courts. Empress Theodora can be seen with her following in the photograph.

221 top left 14th-century buildings and the 18th-century Palazzo dell'Orologio line the large and long Piazza del Popolo, one of the centers of life in Ravenna.

221 top right The Tomb of Galla Placidia was built to hold the remains of the Empress in the 5th century. The inside is decorated with mosaics of great beauty.

223 center The uncommonly green dome topped by a red lantern belongs to the cathedral of Trento. The 18th century Fountain of Neptune at the bottom stands in the center of the square overlooked by elegant but austere medieval buildings.

223 bottom Miramare castle is a 15th-century stronghold built over previous medieval forts. It offers a splendid view over the city of Trieste.

THE NORTHEAST:
LAND OF ART AND WORK

222 top left Piazza dei Signori is the civil and artistic center of Vicenza. It contains some of the city's most important monuments, such as the Palladian Basilica, the Loggia del Capitano and the medieval Torre di Piazza.

222 top right The elegant Gothic-Venetian Palazzo del Comune and the harmonious Portico of St. John, over which stands the 15th century Clocktower, close the magnificent Piazza della Libertà in the center of Udine.

222-223 The imposing building on the north side of Piazza delle Erbe in Padua is the Palazzo della Ragione. It was built in the 12th century but was enlarged and enriched at the start of the 14th century.

223 top The Cappella degli Scrovegni is perhaps Padua's most important building. It was built in the 14th century and contains the cycle of 38 frescoes by Giotto telling the Stories of Mary and Christ, which help the.

224-225 *When the lights of the bridges and the city are reflected in the waters of the river Adige at evening, Verona returns to the time of Romeo and Juliet. In fact, Verona is a bustling commercial city of 300,000 inhabitants and rich and lively enough to have earned itself the role of "crossroads of the northeast." The region as a whole has an industrial productivity rate equal to Japan's.*

224 bottom *The Scaliger bridge is a sort of extension of the Castelvecchio, a magnificent example of medieval fortification built by Cangrande della Scala on the banks of the Adige and incorporating ancient buildings probably of Roman origin. The bridge has three crenellated arches—like the fort—in the Ghibelline style; it connects Castelvecchio to Piazza Arsenale in Borgo Trento. The fortress today houses the Civic Art Museum with a valuable collection of paintings from the Venetian school.*

225 top right The 1st-century Roman amphitheater is one of the three largest buildings of its sort to reach us almost intact; the other two are the Colosseum in Rome and the amphitheater of Capua. At the time of its construction, its 44 tiers were able to seat 25,000 spectators.

225 bottom right Palazzo Giusti on the far side of Ponte Nuovo is famous for its Italian style gardens, terraces, lookout point, avenues lined with cypress trees and interesting layout. The design of the flowerbeds and the statues give the gardens a classical spirit. There is a beautiful view over Verona from the upper terrace.

VERONA:
TRANQUIL BEAUTY

225 top left Piazza Bra is the heart of Veronese life. The square is dominated by the Roman Arena, one of the symbols of the city, and includes the Liston (a favorite promenade of the Veronese). The busy, old center of Verona is triangular in shape, bounded by a bend in the Adige on two sides and by the Via Roma, Via degli Alpini and Via Pallone on the other.

225 bottom left Stage scenery has altered the interior of the Arena: a production of "Carmen" is being staged, one of the most popular operas with the thousands of opera lovers who flock here every summer.

226 top left Venice is the most incredible city in the world. Daughter of the water, mistress of the seas, it seems to be in unstable balance on that narrow strip of land surrounded by water. Yet, despite its precarious situation, Venice manages to preserve a sort of immutability by means of its unique atmosphere, its extra-ordinary historic and artistic palazzi and other monuments.

226 bottom left The dome of St. Mark's is seen in front of the roofs of the old houses in Campo San Lorenzo and Campo San Zanipolo. Seen from the bell tower in St. Mark's square, Venice is an austere city, rich and severe as befitted the Serenissima.

VENICE:

THE CITY OF THE DOGES

226 top right The Punta della Dogana da Mar (the Customs offices), seen here with the church della Salute, separates the mouth of the Grand Canal from the Giudecca canal. It was in this place, that looks like the bow of a ship, that goods arriving by sea used to be unloaded and charged duty.

226 bottom right The Grand Canal and the Rialto bridge are two points of attraction for the tourists that besiege Venice all year round.

227 The long, narrow shape of the island of Giudecca gave it its original name of Spinalonga (long spine). Once the island had orchards, vineyards and palazzi. In more recent times, the growth of industry has meant it has been built over with public housing. The drop-shaped island of San Giorgio Maggiore can be seen at the top of the picture in the center.

228-229 The story goes that the body of St. Mark was brought to Venice in 828 by Rustico da Torcello and Buono Tribuno da Malamocco, two merchants that had stolen the body from Alexandria in Egypt. The remains were brought to the Doge's chapel. Construction of St. Mark's church started soon after but it retained the status of Doge's chapel until 1807 when it was upgraded to the cathedral of Venice.

228 bottom Not only the façade but also the sides of St. Mark's church provide splendid decoration for the square; Venetians and tourists alike consider St. Mark's square to be the most magnificent "drawing room" in the world.

230-231 The interior of St. Mark's is a treasure of mosaics. In the Dome of the Pentecost (left), the Holy Spirit in the form of a dove descends on the Apostles with tongues of fire. Moments from the life of Christ alternate with holy episodes between the two domes. The Ascension of Christ observed by the twelve apostles, two archangels and the Madonna is illustrated in the dome to the right.

229 top The winged lion is the personification of the patron saint of Venice: aggressive, proud and armed with a sword, the Golden Lion in St. Mark's square was a just representation of the power and grandeur of the Serenissima.

229 center The atrium leading to the basilica is richly decorated with mosaics showing episodes from the Old Testament; these masterpieces amply demonstrate the artistic skills of the Venetians in the 13th century. The multi-colored marble flooring in the basilica uses rare and high quality marbles from Constantinople.

229 bottom The Tetrarchs, better known as the Moors, are part of the cell that holds the Treasure of St. Mark. Probably a Syrian work of the 4th century, it shows the tetrarchs and emperors Diocletian and Maximianus together with Galerius and Constant in an embrace that symbolized the unity of the Roman empire.

232 bottom right Every part of the Ducal Palace seems designed to astonish. An example is the so-called Golden Stairway, initially designed by Sansovino but finished by Scarpagnino in 1559. It was given this name for the richness of its ornamentation in white and gilded stuccowork.

233 top left The Senate Room, which was popularly known as the Room of the Pregadi, was the seat of a formal body of 60 members elected by the Greater Council from among the noblemen who had distinguished themselves in public duties.

233 top right A sculpture depicting the "Drunkenness of Noah," by Lombard masters of the 14th-15th centuries, stands on the corner of the Ducal Palace facing the Paglia bridge.

232-233 and 232 bottom left The Ducal Palace was the seat of government of the Serenissima (Republic of Venice) and so had to represent the power and glory of the city to best possible effect. It was the residence of the Doge but also the seat of the Republic's principal magistratures, the Public Archive and, in some manner, it also performed the functions of the law-courts.

233 bottom left The Room of the Greater Council was the place the Venetian nobles used to make laws and to celebrate more solemn events. The impressive ceiling is covered with gold while the far wall is covered with Tintoretto's enormous fresco of Paradise.

233 bottom right Splendid marble reliefs—or, as in this example, proper sculptures—decorate the front and side façades of the Ducal Palace. A recurring theme is the Lion of St. Mark brandishing his sword or resting a paw on the open book "Pax tibi Marce Evangelista meus" (Peace be to you, Mark, my apostle).

234-235 Rialto bridge reflects the pale evening light over the Grand Canal, the main thoroughfare for gondolas, ferries and motorboats. The first version of the bridge was made in 1175 from wood and rested on boats. After the bridge was destroyed by fire, between 1588-91 architect Antonio da Ponte constructed the stone bridge based on a single arch 91 feet wide and 24 feet high.

234 bottom Ca' d'Oro is the pearl of Gothic Venetian architecture. Its name recalls the gilding which once covered the decorations and marblework. It was designed by the Lombard, Matteo Roverti, and the Venetians, Giovanni and Bartolomeo Bon. Now it is the home of the Giorgio Franchetti Gallery.

*235 top The Benedictine
buildings of San Giorgio Maggiore
are colored by the reddish glow of
sunset. The Palladian church, the
bell tower, the monastery and
their works in marble are the
jewel on the "island of cypress
trees."*

*235 center The blue and white
striped moorings rise from the
Grand Canal like trees in a
submerged forest. In the
background, the splendid palazzi
facing onto the canal draw the
attention toward Rialto bridge.*

*235 bottom The success of
tourism in Venice is based on the
city's setting in the lagoon but this
same water continually invades
the city and is the cause of the
widespread belief that the city is
in constant danger. The
attraction of the city also derives
from the hundreds of islands it is
founded on, the approximately
500 canals that criss-cross it and
the more than 400 bridges that
connect the islands.*

236 top and bottom Gondolas are the unique and magical boats that characterize Venice as much as its canals and bridges. Elegant and festive or rustic and workmanlike, they slip through the water like enchanted black swans under the power of the elegant strokes of the gondolier. The details (in this case the decorations in wrought iron and the waterproofed canvas covering of the prow) illustrate the care and love endowed in their manufacture and use.

236-237 The Grand Canal winds through the city, dividing it into two parts. The colored "column" or "palazzo" moorings that line the canal to berth the gondolas are often decorated with a frieze or coat of arms. They also indicate the boundary of the water belonging to the palazzo outside which they stand.

237 bottom Traditional carpentry tools for making boats and gondolas still exist at San Trovaso. The choice of materials is at least as crucial as the design and the construction itself. For a good quality gondola, eight different types of wood are required: deal, larch, cherry, walnut, elm, oak, lime and mahogany. The shape is decided by the maestro who refers to centuries old designs. They are usually painted black.

237 top Some gondolas wrapped in their waxed covers are moored on the Riva degli Schiavoni after a day's work. The Chiesa della Salute and Punta della Dogana can be seen in the background.

237 center Gondolas are still the best way to explore Venice from its canals. The curves and beauty of this unique means of transport are emphasized by the six toothed iron symbol on the prow, known as the "comb," one tooth for each district of the city.

238-239 *A soft orange light emphasizes the late-Renaissance forms of the church Santa Maria della Salute. It was built as an act of thanksgiving after the plague of 1630 in one of the most attractive places in the city, in front of the dock at St. Mark's. Baldassare Longhena was the architect responsible for the unusual octagonal layout of the church.*

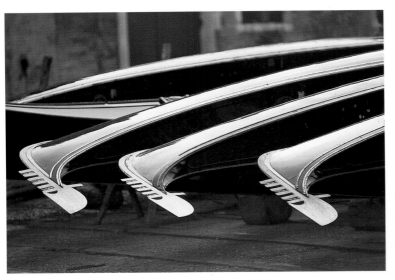

240-241 The lamps glow in the dark and slightly misty air that enfolds St. Mark's square. It is dusk: Venice's "drawing room" is readying itself for another elegant evening and the bars begin to play for their customers of all ages and provenance. This glimpse of the Serenissima from San Giorgio Maggiore is of disquieting beauty.

240 bottom A freezing winter's morning: the low sun reflects coldly in the Grand Canal as it peeps from behind Santa Maria della Salute but the plying of the gondolas, full of tourists, never ceases. A sprinkling of snow on the roofs and domes accentuates the dreamy atmosphere.

241 top left Riva degli Schiavoni is the natural extension of St. Mark's square to the east. This wonderful promenade over the many bridges offers superb views over San Giorgio Maggiore (see photograph) and glimpses of Venice's history; for example, the Bridge of Sighs that connects the Ducal Palace to the Prisons.

241 top right The evening shadows fall over the Clocktower and the Moors, the figures that ring the hours. The tower was built around 1496, probably on the design of Renaissance architect Mauro Coducci who was also responsible for the façade of the church of St. Zachary and the two palazzi, Zorzi and Correr. The Clocktower has an enamelled and gilded face that indicates the time, the phases of the moon and the movement of the sun.

241 bottom left The Caffè Florian is probably the oldest of the bars in St. Mark's square. The luxurious interior, the vaguely middle European atmosphere, the elegance of the furnishings and the style of the staff have always made it one of the city's most exclusive haunts.

241 bottom right With its sophisticated Renaissance architecture and colored marble façade looking onto the Grand Canal, Ca' Dario is a splendid building. Its fame, however, is sinisterly linked to a curse that seems to have been weighed on its owners, often condemned to a violent death.

243 top *During the Fascist era, architect Marcello Piacentini and other famous town-planners worked to give Genoa the air of the maritime capital that the Mussolini government wished it to be. The influence of the reorganisation of that time is still felt in Piazza Vittoria and the district that fronts the railway station at Brignole where old residential areas were replaced by wide roads, squares and monuments.*

243 bottom The lighthouse that shines out to sea in front of the port of Genoa is called simply "La Lanterna" by the Genoese. It is 380 feet high, can be seen from 33 miles away, and has been taken up as the symbol of the city.

LIGURIA:

PORTS OF ART AND COMMERCE

242 top left The sea-facing façade of Palazzo San Giorgio is the first glimpse of Genoa for incoming sailors. The frescoes in the building were painted by Raimondo Sirotti on 17th century designs by Tavarone. The fresco of St. George killing the dragon underlines the religious and sea-going affinity between Genoa and England.

242 top right Via XX Settembre, designed in 1892, is one of Genoa's most important streets. Today it is a parade of elegant shops, cinemas, restaurants and bars; it is always busy and full of traffic.

242-243 The soul of the city of Genoa is its port. Historically, the city's fortunes have depended entirely on its maritime traffic. The port is huge, among the best equipped in Europe, and has for the last few years been undergoing restoration work aimed at recovering buildings in disuse and, in general, an area that risked remaining detached from the rest of the city.

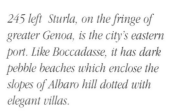

245 left Sturla, on the fringe of greater Genoa, is the city's eastern port. Like Boccadasse, it has dark pebble beaches which enclose the slopes of Albaro hill dotted with elegant villas.

245 top right The line of houses facing the sea and the small, stony beaches are all that there is at Boccadasse, one of Genoa's outlets to the sea. Yet the village is besieged by city residents every weekend and on late summer afternoons.

245 bottom right Porto Maurizio is one of two villages that merged to form Imperia; the other is Oneglia, now an industrial and commercial center. The former is the old center of the city, its medieval buildings stand on a narrow promontory, called locally paraxo.

244-245 The long arterial street, Corso Italia, is lined with sea-bathing facilities. At the end of the Corso stands the village of Boccadasse.

244 bottom left The entire city of Savona is built around its port which was first its pride and later its hope for centuries. Fishing and sail boats today line the old port (photograph).
The entire city of Savona is built around its port which was the pride and hope (after its reconstruction) of the city for centuries. Fishing and sail boats today line the old port (photograph).

244 bottom right The wharves of La Spezia were considered by Napoleon to be part of "the loveliest port in the world." The city is now Italy's largest military port.

247 top Built on the wishes of Maria Luisa of Bourbon, wife of Napoleon, the Teatro Regio is one of Parma's most important buildings. Parma is a rich Emilian city for whom opera is almost a religion.

247 center Famous for a charterhouse that never existed and for the novel by Stendhal, Parma has a wealth of architectural art treasures including the unfinished Palazzo della Pilotta and the baptistery.

247 bottom The church of St. John the Baptist was built in Parma in the 15-16th centuries. It has frescoes by Correggio, wooden choirstalls and, in the Benedictine monastery next door, a beautiful library in the Sala Capitolare (photograph).

BOLOGNA:
IN THE HEART OF EMILIA

246 top left Bologna is the capital of wealthy and industrious Emilia Romagna which is also rich in artistic and architectural treasures. Bononia was founded as an Ibero-Ligurian settlement; it was called Felsina by the Etruscans and Bolonia by the Romans. It experienced a period of prosperity between the 12-15th centuries when the University was established. The historical center and city towers, symbol of the city, are reminders of that flourishing past.

246 top right Asinelli Tower, seen here from Piazza Maggiore, stands at one end of Via Rizzoli. The tower was built during the 12th century for military purposes.

246-247 Palazzi of great beauty face onto Piazza Maggiore (called Piazza Grande by the Bolognese). Two of them are the City Hall, altered in the 15-16th centuries, and the Gothic cathedral of St. Petronius.

248 top St. Michael in Foro is a church in the Pisan-Luccan style from the 12th century with a façade that was added during the 14th century. Its appearance is similar to other Tuscan churches of the same period: tall, slender arcades topped by several rows of small loggias running from the center outward to the bell tower. The triple-nave interior contains magnificent works by Luca della Robbia and Filippino Lippi.

248-249 Lucca is a city with a profusion of art treasures within its walls. It used to be the seat of the Marquis of Tuscany; it was an independent city and maintained its political pre-eminence in Tuscany until the 19th century. It retains few traces of its Roman past but the unmistakable appearance of Piazza del Mercato (see photograph) built over the 2nd-century amphitheater illustrates how much of that era has characterized the modern layout of the city.

249 bottom St. Frediano is a beautiful church in Lucca built around the mid-12th century over an early-Christian basilica of which some remains can be seen inside. The sober façade, uplifted in the 1200s and fitted with a massive crenellated bell tower, is enlivened by a mosaic of the "Ascension of Christ" attributed to the pupils of the Berlinghieri. Despite undergoing heavy restoration last century, it still retains the expressive power and colors typical of the Lucca school in that period. The interior is also worthy of a visit: in particular, the 12th-century purifying-water fountain and the Trenta Chapel with works by Jacopo della Quercia.

LUCCA:
THE WALLED CITY

249 top St. Martin's, Lucca cathedral, was perhaps founded by St. Frediano in the 6th century but the present-day building dates from the end of the 11th and start of the 13th centuries. One of the most beautiful and suggestive works of all time can be seen inside—the funeral monument of Ilaria del Carretto made by Jacopo della Quercia in 1408. The young woman was the wife of Paolo Guinigi, nobleman of the city, and her white marble sculpture that covers the tomb itself shows her in all her beauty.

251 top The statue of Cosimo I de' Medici stands over Piazza dei Cavalieri, the heart of Pisa rebuilt and ennobled by Vasari in the 16th century. Details of the friezes on Palazzo dei Cavalieri can be seen in the background: this too was rebuilt by Vasari and today is the seat of the University.

251 bottom Piazza del Duomo has been renamed Campo dei Miracoli for the extraordinary beauty of its buildings. It is an architectural jewel even in its details as can be seen in these putti. Behind, we see the dome of the cathedral with a remarkable 14th-century loggia.

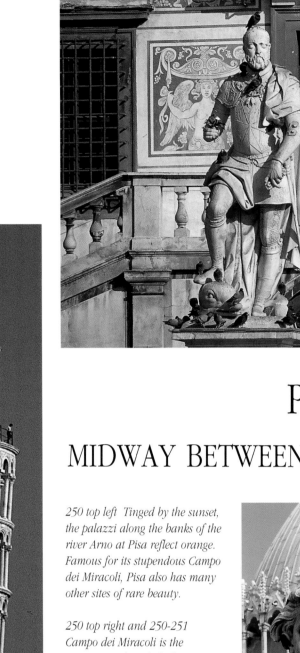

PISA:

MIDWAY BETWEEN ART AND UNIVERSITY

250 top left Tinged by the sunset, the palazzi along the banks of the river Arno at Pisa reflect orange. Famous for its stupendous Campo dei Miracoli, Pisa also has many other sites of rare beauty.

250 top right and 250-251 Campo dei Miracoli is the international symbol of Pisa, city of art and tourism like few others in Italy. This is not just a square where glorious examples of Romanesque architecture are grouped, it is an absolute and perfect set of buildings, even to the contrast of the green of the grass against the white of the marble, in which the imperfection of the Leaning Tower is set. The group of buildings in Campo dei Miracoli (baptistery, cathedral, tower and cemetery) was built over a period from the 11-13th centuries as a monument to God and a testament to the wealth the city had accumulated from shipping.

252 top The church of Santa Croce was begun on the design of Arnolfo di Cambio in 1294 but its façade (designed to complement the original style) was only completed in the 19th century. It is decidedly inferior to the other jewels of Florence. The church plays a unique role in the city and is the Florentine Pantheon where Alfieri, Machiavelli, Michelangelo, Vasari, Rossini and Ugo Foscolo are buried.

252 bottom The detail in the picture shows the beauty of the thin columns and fretwork of the arches in Giotto's bell tower, one of the marvels of Florence. The Tuscan artist only worked on the tower for three years before his death in 1337.

FLORENCE:
THE HEART OF THE RENAISSANCE

252-253 Piazza San Giovanni, better known as Piazza Duomo, is one of two crossroads in Florence: the other is Piazza della Signoria. The buildings it contains (cathedral, bell tower and baptistery) make it a smaller version of the Campo dei Miracoli in Pisa though no less valid artistically. Giotto's bell tower and Brunelleschi's dome dominate the city when seen from any point of view.

253 top left Piazzale Michelangelo on the road to San Miniato al Monte gives a magnificent view of Florence from south of the Arno. The square has a monument to the artist and is one of the tourists' favorite stopping off spots for photographs of the city.

253 top right Ponte Vecchio crosses the Arno near Palazzo Pitti and connects the Boboli Gardens with Piazza della Signoria. It is lined on both sides by craft shops and goldsmiths.

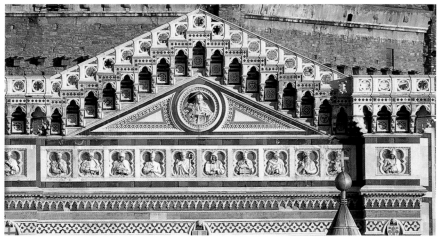

254 top left Santa Maria del Fiore is a masterpiece of Italian Gothic architecture. Work began on top of the site of the previous cathedral in 1296 based on the designs of Arnolfo di Cambio. When the architect died, others were employed on the project, including Giotto and Brunelleschi. The façade was rebuilt in the 19th century but several doors are the originals from the 14th century, for example, those of the bell tower.

254 bottom left Palazzo Medici-Riccardi, of which we see a glimpse of the courtyard, was built during the Renaissance by Michelozzo. It used to be the residence of Lorenzo the Magnificent and today houses the offices of the Prefecture.

254 top right Santa Maria del Fiore, the baptistery and Giotto's bell tower form an architectural set of buildings that is famous around the world. Together, the monuments combine the best of western architecture between 11-14th centuries. The greatest artists of the age worked on them, including Arnolfo di Cambio, Brunelleschi, Giotto and Ghiberti.

254 bottom right Santa Croce is the Franciscan basilica that was founded in 1228 and remodelled several times since. The entire structural basis and majestic interior of the original Gothic temple, praised by author Ugo Foscolo in his Sepolcri, still remain.

255 Palazzo Vecchio, started in 1299, in the 19th century was the seat of the government and the Chamber of Deputies in the Kingdom of Italy, now it is home to Florence City Council.

256 left Among the superb monuments that adorn Piazza della Signoria, there is the famous "Biancone" (the fountain of Neptune's chariot), a late 16th-century work by Bartolomeo Ammannati. This artist and architect also collaborated on the expansion of Palazzo Pitti.

256 top right The original version of Michelangelo's David stands in the Galleria dell'Accademia but an identical copy is still shown in Piazza della Signoria next to the entrance to Palazzo Vecchio. The statue is considered by experts to be an important work in the tormented career of the artist able to produce sculptural, pictorial and architectural masterpieces and who was the real precursor of the Baroque period.

256 bottom right The church of Santa Maria Novella is the first work of art seen by visitors arriving in Florence by train. It was begun in the mid-12th century and is a marvelously harmonious example of Italian Gothic architecture. The arches that adorn the façade were designed by Leon Battista Alberti, one of the masters of the Renaissance. Geometrical designs and floral decorations merge into a gentle classical motif.

256-257 Florence was founded on the banks of the river Arno and developed into a trove of artistic treasures. Cities like Florence are capable of producing what is called the "Stendhal Syndrome," i.e. swooning induced in some people when confronted by the beauty and perfection of outstanding artistic creations.

257 bottom Boboli gardens were created on the wishes of Eleonora, wife of Cosimo I. They are Florence's most important park. Their layout reflects late-Renaissance style with grottoes, avenues, fountains, large grassy areas and shaped hedges. The highest terraces of the gardens give marvelous views over the city.

258 Experts aver that it was Botticelli (Sandro Filipepi) who was responsible for the development of pictorial art from the 15th to the 16th century. Influenced originally by Pollaiolo and Verrocchio, Botticelli turned the refinement of the Medici environment with which he was familiar into clean, sinuous lines made vital with the use of transparent colors. Some of his works were allegorical like Spring or The Birth of Venus. Spring was a great work from his early period that used fluid, wave-like lines to create grace, beauty and lightness, symbolized by the movements of the veiled dancers. Struck by a profound religious crisis in 1490, after Savonarola's preaching, Botticelli infused his paintings with a greater sense of drama reflecting the unease and conflicts of the period in which he lived.

259 The musicality and delicacy that pervaded Spring four years earlier were also to be seen in The Birth of Venus of 1482. The same age as Lorenzo de Medici, Botticelli could not but be affected by the illuminated spirit of "the Magnificent" and, in his two most famous masterpieces, both commissioned by Lorenzo's cousin, the attempt to erase all materialism to make space for abstraction is evident.

The philosophy underlying Botticelli's 'Medici' period was Neo-Platonism which preached the need to alienate the body in order to liberate the spirit. The beauty of Venus in the picture was the means by which the spirit could be lightened of every material burden and led toward divinity. Both paintings can be seen in the Uffizi Gallery, one of the world's most important art collections.

260 top *The Madonna Rucellai is by Duccio di Buoninsegna. It was painted in 1285 and is hung in the Uffizi. This picture and a subsequent painting, Majesty from 1308, are considered Duccio's most important works in which he was able to bring together and harmonize Gothic and Byzantine styles.*

260 bottom *Early works by Leonardo da Vinci were based on religious themes. The genius of the artist is already evident in his Annunciation of 1475 in the depth of the perspective emphasized by the vagueness of the background, the precision of the decorative details and the use of gentle colors.*

260-261 *Simone Martini of the Siena school painted this "Annunciation," also in the Uffizi, in 1333 shortly before leaving Italy. The painting illustrates a search for spiritual beauty by means of purity of shapes and luminosity of colors.*

263 Siena cathedral is lined with white and black marble, a flash of Gothic architecture in the center of a medieval, brick city. The artistically grandiose temple (shown by the beauty of the Romanesque bell tower (above) and the exuberant façade (below) was to become the transept of an immense church if the plans of the 14th century City Council had gone ahead. Unfortunately, events in the life of the city and the geological situation brought the project to a halt but the importance of the arcades of the unfinished building, now occupied by the Museum of the Metropolitan Opera, is clear to see.

SIENA:

A PEARL AMONG THE HILLS

262 top left The Palazzo Pubblico, built between 1288-1342, is one of Siena's most original and elegant examples of non-religious Gothic architecture. It features three brick sections with Guelph crenellations. It stands in the shadow of the Torre del Mangia, designed toward the mid-14th century by Minuccio and Francesco di Rinaldo.

262 top right Siena cathedral was the fruit of the work of many artists from the mid-13th century. The interior and exterior have in common the patterns in two-colored marble and enormous decorative richness.

262-263 Piazza del Campo is a reddish shell reached through a maze of alleys. It has a natural slope. It is the center of Siena and the site of the twice yearly Palio horse-race, a tradition at the heart of what it means to be Sienese.

264 top The rich trading town of San Gimignano developed on the Via Francigena, the most important route during the Middle Ages. The richest families built houses with towers, for defensive reasons and for status—the higher the tower, the greater the status of the family. During its richest period, San Gimignano had 65 towers but today only 8 remain. The photograph shows Piazza della Cisterna where the inhabitants have drawn drinking water for over 800 years.

SAN GIMIGNANO:
CITY OF THE TOWERS

264 bottom A cycle of frescoes by Barna da Siena, Stories from the New Testament, decorates the right hand nave of the Collegiata, San Gimignano's 12th-century cathedral. The church was also decorated by other artists such as Taddeo di Bartolo, Benozzo Gozzoli, Bartolo di Fredi and Domenico Ghirlandaio.

264-265 The view of San Gimignano from the hills of Val d'Elsa. The towers, like early skyscrapers, are evidence of the wealth the medieval town accumulated trading local products: Vernaccia wine, saffron and decorated leather products.

265 top The History of St. Fina is a cycle of late 15th-century frescoes in San Gimignano cathedral by Domenico Ghirlandiao (Death on the left, Burial on the right). The frescoes, like the architecture by Giuliano and Benedetto da Maiano, are artistic jewels.

266 left Despite its severity and lack of ornamentation, the cathedral of Arezzo is unquestionably majestic. The steps lead to a standard three-nave interior decorated with frescoes and large windows. The left-hand nave has a famous fresco by Piero della Francesca, Mary Magdalene, painted in the 16th century.

266 top right The ruins of the Cistercian Abbey of St. Galgano stand in the countryside between Siena and Arezzo. It was founded by a noble who retired here as a hermit but by the early 15th century the building had already begun to fall down leaving the naves open to the sky.

AREZZO:

IN THE LAND OF GOLD

266 bottom right Piazza Grande in Arezzo, like Piazza del Campo in Siena, has a natural slope. It is surrounded by the city's most important buildings: the Palazzo del Tribunale, Palazzo della Fraternita' dei Laici and the Palazzo delle Logge, this last designed by Giorgio Vasari.

267 The 13th-century church of St. Francis looks over the square of the same name in the old walled city of Arezzo. The church is to all intents an art museum: it contains the extraordinary cycle of frescoes by Piero della Francesca of The Story of the True Cross which gathers all the themes and forms of Renaissance painting into one work.

269 bottom left Situated on the edge of a large green hollow, Gubbio unites the natural beauty of its district with artistic masterpieces and monuments from the Middle Ages. Via dei Consoli and Via Baldassini are the ancient roads that pass through the town and are the sites of the most important buildings: the church of St. John the Baptist, the Consuls' Palace (respectively in the picture), the Ducal Palace and the church of St. Francis.

269 top right Urbino is joint provincial capital with Pesaro and a jewel that lies in the hills of Marche. The old center is ringed by ancient walls and an incomparable treasure of Renaissance architecture.

269 bottom right Construction of the Ducal Palace in Urbino was started in 1444 by Maso di Bartolomeo and then transformed many times. Inside there is a "courtyard of honor" which is considered the highest expression of civil Renaissance architecture.

UMBRIA AND MARCHE:
THE GREEN HEART OF ITALY

268 Standing on a hill over a wide Umbrian valley, Spoleto has maintained its appearance of an important medieval town (it used to be the capital of a Longobard duchy before being passed to the Catholic church). Its cathedral was built at the end of the 12th century and partially retouched in the 17th. Its severe Romanesque façade is original while the bell tower dates from the 16th century.

269 top left Todi has also managed to maintain its noble medieval appearance. Piazza del Popolo was built over the original Roman forum and is one of Italy's most beautiful squares. Facing onto it are the Priors' Palace, the People's Palace, the Captain's Palace and, from the top of a symbolic flight of steps, the Gothic cathedral, begun in the 11th century and completed between the 12th-16th centuries.

270 top The history of the city of Orvieto, built on a steep hill of tufa, goes back to before the classical era. It was inhabited long before the Etruscans took it over, then passed to the Romans and then flourished during the Middle Ages with the name of Urbs Vetus. Its medieval wealth is still apparent in the artistic heritage of the two squares, Piazza Duomo and Piazza del Popolo.

ORVIETO:

THE CITY THAT STANDS ON TUFA

270 bottom Resurrection of the Flesh is one of a cycle of Biblical frescoes by Luca Signorelli in the Chapel of St. Brizio in Orvieto cathedral. Signorelli was a pupil of the two masters, Piero della Francesca and Pollaiolo. The cycle was painted between 1499-1503 and also includes Stories of the Antichrist, The End of Humanity, Hell and Heaven. During his long artistic career, Signorelli was also responsible for the fresco in the Sistine Chapel of the Testament and Death of Moses.

271 Orvieto cathedral was built between 1290-1330 following the most classical dictates of Italian Gothic architecture. Its façade, designed by Maitani and finished in the 16th century, is heavily decorated with sculptures and mosaics. Pinnacles, loggias, columns and delicate marble filigree render the cathedral visually interesting and confer on it a sense of lightness. The interior and the museum hold masterpieces by Simone Martini, Signorelli and Andrea Pisano.

272 top Perugia was originally a Neolithic settlement. It then became an independent city-state and is now a rich, industrial city. Yet it retains traces of its past in the layout of the town and in its principal buildings. Perugia's artistic heritage is mainly to be seen in the Oratory of St. Bernadino, the city's most important Renaissance building, a 15th century masterpiece by Agostino di Duccio.

PERUGIA, ASSISI AND NORCIA:
ON THE TRAIL OF ST. FRANCIS

272 center The basilica of St. Francis of Assisi is one of the Christian world's most famous churches. It was probably designed by Brother Elia, spiritual son of St. Francis and his second in command of the Order. The church was begun in 1228 and consecrated in 1253.

272 bottom The statue of St. Benedict, born in Norcia, seems to protect the square named after him. In the background stands the cathedral built in 1560.

272-273 Assisi is a city of remarkable cultural, environmental and artistic resources; it is also a place of pilgrimage for followers of the Christian faith.

273 top Meetings of Perugia City Council used to take place in the Sala delle Udienze in the Collegio dei Cambi (left) and the Sala dei Notari in the Palazzo dei Priori (right). The first was decorated by Perugino in the late 15th century; the second by Roman masters who were already working on the church of St. Francis of Assisi.

274-275 The basilica of St. Francis contains two churches, the Lower and the Upper, decorated with frescoes by Giotto and Cimabue. The lower of the two seems like a church in a crypt and acts as a foundation for the upper one. They have low ceilings, wide cross vaults and stupendous 14th-century decorations. The vault is embellished with allegories of the three virtues—Poverty, Chastity and Obedience—and the fresco of Triumph of St. Francis by Giotto and his school.

274 bottom The center of the single nave in the Lower Church of St. Francis of Assisi is magnificent yet not heavy with decoration. Contributors to its wall-frescoes were Andrea da Bologna, the so-called Maestro of St. Francis, Giotto, Cimabue and Pietro Lorenzetti.

275 top right The left transept of the Lower Church of St. Francis has frescoes by Pietro Lorenzetti: The Crucifixion (photograph), Madonna with Child and SS. Francis and John, Descent from the Cross and Deposition in the Sepulchre. Clearly influenced by Giotto and his school, Lorenzetti was one of the masters of 14th-century Italian painting.

275 bottom right Pietro Lorenzetti painted this Entrance to Jerusalem during the 1320s. The new and important role of scenic elements is evident, in particular the details of the Gothic architecture that symbolizes Jerusalem. The fresco is part of the cycle that decorates the left transept of the lower church.

275 left The Chapel of St. Martin in the lower church was entirely decorated by Simone Martini, one of the precursors of international Gothic style. The fresco, St. Mary Magdalene and St. Catherine of Alexandria was painted in 1317 along with the icons of other saints and wall paintings at the entrance to the chapel. Also present in the chapel is the cycle, The History of St. Martin.

276 top left *The cycle of frescoes by Giotto in the nave of the upper church of St. Francis of Assisi was begun in 1296. Their subject (The Life of St. Francis) and the magnificence of their execution make them an absolute masterpiece of pre-Renaissance Italian painting. The lack of symbolism and the straightforwardness of the scenes reflect the social changes of the times: a class of craftsmen and merchants had been created which required spiritual education but linked to the objects of everyday existence. Indeed it is the commonplace that is the main element throughout all 28 episodes in the life of the saint (whose Order was at the height of its influence at the time): Francis is shown as a contemporary of Giotto—solid and dignified—and not at all the poor ingenuous he is portrayed as traditionally.*

276 bottom left *Like other well-known episodes in the cycle of St. Francis, including Preaching to the Birds and Miracle of the Spring, this Gift of a Cloak to a Poor Man is characterized by a high degree of realism for the era in which it was painted. St. Francis is shown in a faithful reproduction of the environment Giotto lived in, shown by the architecture of the town in the background. There is little room here for symbolism or mysticism; all is related directly to the reality of the late 13th century.*

276 right *The splendid cross vault of the Upper Church contains superb geometrical and floral decorations that frame the frescoes. They exemplify the magnificence with which the basilica of St. Francis of Assisi was ornamented. The frescoes of the four Doctors of the Church— St. Jerome, St. Augustine, St. Gregory and St. Ambrose—are attributed to Giotto as a young man and are believed to have been painted around 1293.*

276-277 The Upper Church of St. Francis of Assisi was built around the mid-13th century, the fabbrica of the religious complex was inaugurated two years before the death of the saint in 1226. As soon as the work was begun, the city became the heart of the Franciscan order. The friary contains two churches, one on top of the other. The lower church contains the tomb of St. Francis and therefore soon became a popular place of pilgrimage as well as being a place of sanctuary. The upper church was built using the lower one as a foundation; one of its purposes was its use for preaching (a crucial role of the Franciscan doctrine based on poverty and continual contact with the poorer members of society) and liturgical activities in general. The two churches each have a single nave, supported by long cylindrical beams and flying buttresses. The beautiful cross vaults and apse of the upper church (see photograph) are decorated with frescoes by Cimabue, now partially damaged. Besides taking many lives, the 1997 earthquake wrought incalculable artistic and historical harm which will require long and painstaking restoration.

279 The Galleria Umberto I stands in front of the Teatro San Carlo near Piazza Plebiscito, the center of Naples. It was built at the end of the 19th century and resembles the Galleria in Milan aesthetically and in layout. It is covered by an airy glass dome on an octagonal base (top) fronted by an enormous entrance with colonnade and portico (bottom). Like many other buildings in the old center, the Galleria contributes to the status of Naples as an international city. The history of Naples was for a long time linked to the fortunes of the Bourbons, one of Europe's most important dynasties.

NAPLES:

THE QUEEN OF THE BAY

278 top right Castel dell'Ovo was built in the 13th century by the port of Santa Lucia. It is one of Naples' most famous buildings and a natural end to the promenade along the sea-front.

278-279 Mergellina at the foot of Posillipo at sunset. The sea-front of Via Caracciolo rings the bay; in the distance, Castel dell'Ovo is hidden in the evening mist.

BARI, BRINDISI AND LECCE:
IN THE HEART OF BAROQUE PUGLIA

281 top left The port of Bari stretches between the old city and the Trade Fair area. The port is equipped for high volumes of international commercial shipping and pleasure boats.

281 top right The importance of Bari's past can be seen in the old city, laid out during the Middle Ages. The clear division between the old and new cities was the result of expansion during the Napoleonic era.

280 top The current cathedral in Brindisi is an 18th-century restoration of the previous 12th-century Romanesque church. It stands in Piazza Duomo in the heart of the city with the Loggia Balsamo, Portico dei Cavalieri and Palazzo Vescovile. The old city is surrounded on three sides by the sea and was the center of an important port area during the Roman era.

280 bottom Santa Croce is Lecce's fullest example of Baroque architecture. It was built in the 16-17th centuries with a splendid façade filled with decorations of all kinds in which the contributions of the different sculptors commissioned during the various phases of work can be recognized.

280-281 Regional capital of Puglia and modern and dynamic city, Bari is the third largest city in south Italy and sees itself as a bridge between the east and west of the Adriatic. The old city (see photograph) is wedged in the sea between the port and the modern city.

282 top left Palermo is the second largest city in south Italy. Despite dramatic growth after World War II, the Sicilian capital has managed to maintain the heritage of its historic and artistic glory. It had been inhabited even before it became a Punic city called Ziz but then passed into the hands, in turn, of the Romans, the Byzantines, the Saracens and the Normans. Clear evidence has been left of the city's centuries long domination by the Spanish.

282 center left The church of St. John of the Hermits stands in Via dei Benedettini. It is one of Palermo's most celebrated buildings. It was built on the wishes of Ruggero II in 1142 during Norman rule and shows clear eastern influences in the red domes and cloister.

282 bottom left The fountain in Piazza Pretoria was built for Don Pedro de Toledo and was bought by the Senate of Palermo in 1578, then erected in the square.

SICILY:
FROM MAGNA GRECIA TO THE THIRD MILLENIUM

282 top right Palermo is a city of culture that has never stopped growing and which offers the visitor many surprises. For example, a bronze quadriga by local sculptor Mario Rutelli looks out from the top of the Politeama Garibaldi, built in the second half of the 19th century by architect Damiani Almeyda; some of the rich ornamentation of the façade is visible on the frieze.

282 bottom right The masterpiece of Norman architecture, Monreale cathedral, was built between 1172-89 on the edge of the city. The cloister is particularly richly decorated with 228 twin columns either sculpted or lined with mosaics. The columns support ogival arches showing Arab influences.

283 The 17th-century sanctuary of St. Rosalia stands on the slopes of Mount Pellegrino with its slender towers pointing to the Sicilian sky.

284-285 Mount Etna dominates the city of Catania. In the photograph, it overlooks a building in late 19th-century style that stands in the Bellini Garden. The garden is the city's most important park and is home to animals and centuries old trees. It used to house a couple of elephants which were so loved by the residents that an elephant was chosen as a symbol for the city.

284 bottom Etna seems to peep over the port of Catania. The port has been one of the two engines that have brought wealth to the city, one of the most industrious and active in Sicily. The other is the ancient university.

285 top The stately city of Siracusa came into being in ancient times, originally founded by Corinthian settlers. It experienced alternating periods of turbulence and prosperity up until the year 1000 when it fell under Norman domination but, like the rest of Sicily, it was conquered by the kingdom of Aragon during the 14th century. The cycle of invasions and dominations however did not destroy the great Greek and Roman monuments which have turned the area into an important archeological site.

285 center The small town of Piazza Armerina on the slopes of the Erei mountains is a holiday resort and archeological site of major importance. The center is dominated by the 17th-century cathedral built over the remains of a 15th-century church. Not far from the town, the marvellous floor mosaics of Villa Romana del Casale can be seen, considered an extraordinary document of Roman art and customs.

285 bottom At nearly 3,280 feet altitude, Enna is the highest provincial capital in Europe. It has attractive views over the Dittaino valley and inland Sicily. Originally a Byzantine stronghold, Enna flourished briefly during the Middle Ages and under Aragon domination. Its most important buildings, the Lombardy Castle and the cathedral, date from that period.

286 left Cefalù owes its name to the rock that stands over it, which from certain points of view resembles a head. The town was founded during the Greek era and did well under the Normans who left it a solemn monument— the cathedral. Built on the wishes of Ruggero II, it is one of Sicily's most beautiful buildings and dominates the skyline of the town.

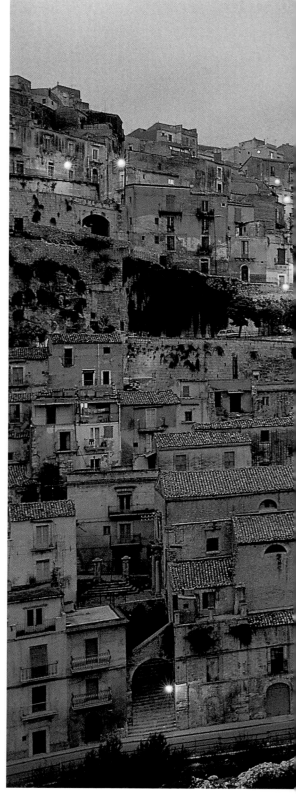

286-287 The Baroque palazzi illuminated at dawn stand over the dark roofs of Ibla. This town was completely destroyed by the 1693 earthquake and rebuilt according to the taste then in vogue. Today it is almost a part of the city of Ragusa, built on the hill behind, and the two are connected by a series of bridges and steps.

287 bottom Erice stands on a rise of 2,600 feet near Trapani. It is internationally known for its Majorana Science Center. It looks like an intact medieval town with houses in the Arab-Spanish style, each with a patio. Among its monuments stands the Castle of Venus, so named because it was built over an ancient sanctuary to Venus.

288 top The church of the Holy Trinity in Saccargia, south of Sassari, was founded in 1116. It is considered a masterpiece of Sardinian Romanesque architecture. It was given to the Camaldolo monks by Costantino di Torres who had it built in "Tuscan" style by Pisan stonemasons at the end of the 12th century. The placename means "the Friesian cow" in honour of a cow that was supposed to have knelt in front of an invisible spirit in this area.

288 center The Bastion of St. Rémy is one of the scenes decorating the castle in Cagliari built in Neo-classical style at the end of the 19th century.

SARDINIA:

THE TREAUSURES OF THE PROUD ISLAND

288 bottom Piazza d'Italia and Piazza Duomo are the two centers of life in Sassari. The Provincial Council has its offices in Palazzo Provinciale in Piazza d'Italia.

288-289 The capital, Cagliari, is Sardinia's most important city. The original settlements were colonised by the Phoenicians and Carthaginians. Its history is made up of a cycle of invasions and dominations but it experienced a period of particular splendour under the kingdom of Aragon and the Spaniards. The city's most important buildings, grouped in the acropolis, all date from those eras.

289 top Alghero owes its name to the abundance of seaweed around its foundations ("alguer" is the Catalan word for seaweed). It is a beautiful city on the north-western coast of Sardinia. Founded in the 12th century, it has an original church St. Michael, (right) with a dome covered in colored majolica tiles.

Festivals, traditions and folklore of an ancient people

Songs sung during harvest time and those sung on the festival of the patron saint; the ceremonies that signal the end of the farming year or the start of spring; the competitions and contests between rival quarters of a city; parades, processions during Carnival and Holy Week, exorcisms, spells and counter-spells. To subsume these topics and all the others in which a people manifests its collective spirit and culture in one collective noun, W.J. Thoms, the English antiquarian, coined the term "folklore" in 1846.

In Italy, this word takes on even greater meaning than in other countries for geographical, social and historical reasons. Its position in the center of the Mediterranean and its connection to the heart of Europe have made it a land open to all surrounding peoples and civilisations. The richness and variety of its scenery, its historical capacity to produce culture, its having been the cradle of Christianity and Latinism but also, in large measure and for many hundreds of years, a country of peasant subsistence, have give the peoples that lived here an unusual capacity to assimilate different mentalities, experiences and cultural expressions, to fuse them with their own, adapt them to their own spirit and to express them in authentic and original ways in its own folklore.

Today Italy is one of the major industrial powers in the world, but its farming roots are still very much evident and influential. The ancient ceremonies can still be seen in the repetition of the thousand celebrations each year, though not perhaps understood very deeply, that so charmed travelers to Italy in the 19th century such as Goethe.

290 bottom right Carnival in the mountains, such as the one in the valley of Gran San Bernardo, is based on unchanged customs dating back to ancient times.

290 top right and 291 The traditional costumes of the valley of Gressoney are brightly colored and embroidered. The stiff head-covering for women ends with ribbons sewn with gold thread.

290 left The largest and healthiest cows are the winners in the "Battle of the Queens" that takes place on the third Sunday of October in Aosta Valley. The award is contested at the final at Croix Noir among successful contestants from the knock-out stages, all of whom must be in calf. The most impressive cows confront one another and the ones that take a step backward are eliminated. The final winner is covered with garlands of flowers and paraded.

292-293 The contest is the culminating moment of the Sartiglia in Oristano. It begins with the dressing of the rider by priestesses who then lift him onto his horse to ensure his feet do not touch the ground. He then blesses the crowd with a bunch of violets and periwinkles while the crowd in turn showers him with corn and flowers.

292 top left and 293 top All the riders in costume in the procession during the Sartiglia wear female masks and men's clothing. The cumponidori however is androgynous and wears both women's and men's clothing. After the contest, in which the riders have to skewer a ring in a star with their swords or lances, the procession moves off to an area where the town wall once stood and where two

towers remain. Here they display a series of daring acrobatic feats in what was once the moat. A group of three or four horses gallop side by side while the riders—either two to a horse or standing on the horse's back— perform acrobatics to the sound of trumpets and roll of drums. These equestrian tricks were believed in the past to strengthen the walls by creating a magic circle around them.

Spring representing the awakening of nature and the season of love is the spirit of many ancient popular and traditional ceremonies while marriage services which reflect rustic fertility rites often are part of many public festivals. Several of these, for example the *Sartiglia* of Oristano in Sardinia, repeat interesting ancient initiation rites. The *Sartiglia* is held on the last Sunday and Tuesday of Carnival. The festival begins with a long parade in brightly colored medieval costume in ancient Spanish or Sardinian styles. Then a sort of jousting competition takes place where the riders have to run their sword or a lance through a star-shaped ring hanging from a cord while at the gallop. Unlike other forms of Carnival which are generally comical or satirical, the *Sartiglia* is calm, almost solemn. Masks are used purely to indicate theatrical or ritual characters and the most important moment of the ceremony is the strictly ceremonial investiture of the *componidori* (the principal rider whose task it is to skewer the star first) but the whole procedure maintains complex and allegorical meanings. The young man is taken to a setting decked out with branches, leaves and flowers and is prepared by a group of women known as *massaieddas* under the guidance of a senior woman known as *sa massaia manna*. The young man is made to sit on a seat placed on a table and, from that moment on, may not touch the ground with his feet. He is dressed by the younger women with a white shirt decorated with colored ribbons over his own costume. His face is made up like a woman's, a wedding veil is placed over his head and, on top of

that, a black top hat. He is then carried onto his horse and given a bunch of violets and periwinkles to hold; the bunch of flowers is known as *sa pippia de maiu* (young girl of May) and is a symbol of male and female together. The *componidori* then blesses the crowd as he is showered in grain and flowers. Finally, he is ready to ride to the jousting ring with the other riders whose faces are also made up like women's but who wear men's costumes. The result of the jousting tournament is taken as an omen for the new farming year while the outcomes of other cavalcades have no significance and are considered simply tests of skill. When this phase of the festival is finished, the procession moves on to another site for exhibitions of expertise and daring. Groups of three or four riders gallop side by side while riders acrobatically move from one mount to another to the accompaniment of trumpets and the roll of drums. Italian folklore has many examples of worship of the solstices which have remained at the root of Christian festivals in December. December 25th, the birth of Christ, also used to be a Roman festival. Magical rites, divination and Christian religion are mixed in representations that celebrate the nativity and which, in some places, involve processions of hundreds of people with sheep, horses, oxen and pigs to the place of the birth.

292 bottom left, 292 bottom right, 293 bottom The modern version of the Sartiglia dates from Spanish domination of Sardinia and its name probably comes from the Castilian word sortija meaning ring (what the riders have to catch on their lances while at the gallop). The last Monday of Carnival the celebration, called Sartiglietta, is reserved for children who represent the adult version in every detail.

294 top, 294-295, 295 left At
Carnival time, Venice is
transformed into an animated
stage filled with people in fancy
dress of all types. The costumes are
curious and elegant and often
created with great care and
knowledge. Huge numbers of
people in the lanes and squares
attend shows and concerts while
more reserved parties take place in
the palazzi that face onto the
Grand Canal.

The festival that more than any other
fuses pagan rites, Christian spirituality,
magic, exorcism, history, legend, playfulness
and death is Carnival. The roots of Carnival
go back to the Roman *lupercali,* rituals that
took place in mid-February in which the
luperci, young men consecrated to the god
Pan, ran nude holding the skins of sacrificed
goats that they used to lash sterile women.
This was a propitiatory ceremony to
celebrate the end of a period of sterility
(winter) and the onset of fertility (spring).

This pagan rite did not disappear with the advent of Christianity but was transformed and became part of the new religious and cultural context. During Carnival, ugly puppets and masks are paraded (representing winter) which get battered, damaged and are ultimately destroyed; alternatively, symbolic characters (scapegoats for the excesses that take place during Carnival celebrations or during the year) are burned.

For the hundreds of years between

medieval times and the 18th century, Carnival represented the negation of constituted order and the principles that governed social behavior; it was "the world turned upside-down" in which there were no prohibitions and where the exchange of roles between the governed and the governors was permitted. At one time in Rome, Carnival was celebrated by a carriage of mad people touring the city with the keys to the asylum in their hands. In many places, mask wearers were allowed to enter houses without identifying themselves; another custom was to sprinkle flour and soot over passers-by (today that mixture has happily become confetti). Modern day Carnival is celebrated throughout the towns and villages of Italy with different festivals and ceremonies. The most well-known are those of Venice and Viareggio. Carnival in Venice brings great crowds in masks and fancy dress into the lanes, campiellos and

squares for an entire week. Dressing up has always been central to Carnival in this city. Venetians, whether courtesans, beggars, debtors, ruffians, rich or poor, have always loved putting on their masks to escape identification even outside Carnival time. This habit became so common and was considered so dangerous that a law was passed in 1268 prohibiting the use of masks at any other than the Carnival period. The festival still follows the ancient ritual with the flight of the dove in St. Mark's to open proceedings, then the parade of boats on the Grand Canal on the Saturday before Easter and the burning of Pantaloon (a character representing miserliness) on Shrove Tuesday in St. Mark's Square.

The Carnival in Viareggio is the most spectacular in Italy where 16 floats process through the town inspired by Italian and international politics; this follows the Carnival tradition of making fun of those in power. Besides these there is a group of fifteen or so similarly masked revellers and others in varying costumes. The first Carnival celebration took place in Viareggio in 1873 when the place was a large naval town. The procession was made up of decorated carts and small allegorical constructions, later came carts dedicated to the triumph of progress and universal peace and, finally, the mood turned to political satire. The first parades wound along Via Regia which stretched inland from the sea but in 1921 the route was changed to the seafront. During that period the locals learned to use papier-mâché which was of great effect in producing unusual effects. A profession was born, that of the *carristi* (cart-decorators), at which they are still masters.

295 right The Carnival in Viareggio was started in 1873 as a public masquerade. Now it has the largest parade of floats in Italy on which the locals work the whole year round. When the floats parade down the sea-front, it is a marvelous sight: some are 65 feet high and 33 wide. The symbolic figure of Viareggio's Carnival is King Burlamacco, as fat as Falstaff and just as cheerful, leads the procession often accompanied by an actress or television star in costume. Other events that take place during Carnival are feasts in the different quarters of the town, gastronomic fairs, theatrical and puppet shows, exhibitions, sports competitions, concerts and open air dancing.

296 top and 297 bottom right
The first palio in Siena, dedicated
to the Madonna of Provenzano,
takes place on July 2nd. The
second, dedicated to the Madonna
of the Assumption, is held on
August 16th. The Madonna is the
patron of the city, which has been
known as the civitas Virginis (city
of the Virgin) since 2 September
1260 when Siena officially gave
her its allegiance by deed. To
experience the Palio in Siena to

the full, the visitor must arrive in
the city at least four days before the
race and stay a few more
afterward. This allows time to
enjoy the preparations, the
ceremonies (such as the blessing of
the horse in the church in each
city quarter), open air dinners for
the whole district at enormous
tables, and the dazzling procession
in Piazza del Campo that
accompanies the palio itself (the
portrait of the Madonna) or cencio
as it is called in Siena.

296-297 and 297 left During the
race the only thing that matters is
winning. There are no rules at the
Palio and it is not unusual for
riders to be bribed by rival
quarters. Only ten riders of the
seventeen quarters can take part in
the race and they are selected on a
rotating basis. The seven excluded
the previous time race plus three
chosen at random.

297 top right and center The
ceremony at the beginning of the
race is complex; it is directed by a
starter who attempts to line the
horses up. Once the off is given and
the tension rises even further, the
jockeys have to circle the piazza
three times. The race only lasts 80
seconds during which anything can
happen—the jockeys might use their
whips on the horses of their rivals to
distract them and even on other
jockeys! Blocking rivals or pushing
them toward the barriers is quite
legal and if a jockey falls, his horse
can go on to win riderless.

The Italian August Bank Holiday
(ferragosto) is rooted in Roman tradition. It is
the modern version of the *feriae Augusti,* the
celebrations for Augustus and the time for
holidays. In Italy it is traditional to celebrate this
day with competitions, tests of skill, processions
and parades of carts that carry gifts to the
churches. The Palio between the quarters of the
city of Siena is the most well-known example of
ferragosto celebrations. It goes back to
equestrian sports practiced by the Etruscans,
which continued through the Middle Ages.
Today the passion of the medieval tussles are
still as frenzied as they have ever been and the
ceremony involved in the presentation of the
horses, the course trials in Piazza del Campo,
the noisy dinners before and after the race and
the processions in costume is no less
diminished. Whoever wins (even a horse alone
if the rider has been thrown) is presented with
the portrait of the Madonna (palio), which is
then carried into church for a thanksgiving *Te
Deum.* The festival finishes in the victor's
quarter with a feast with the winning horse in
the place of honor.

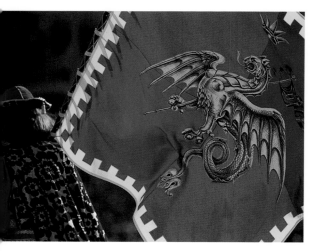

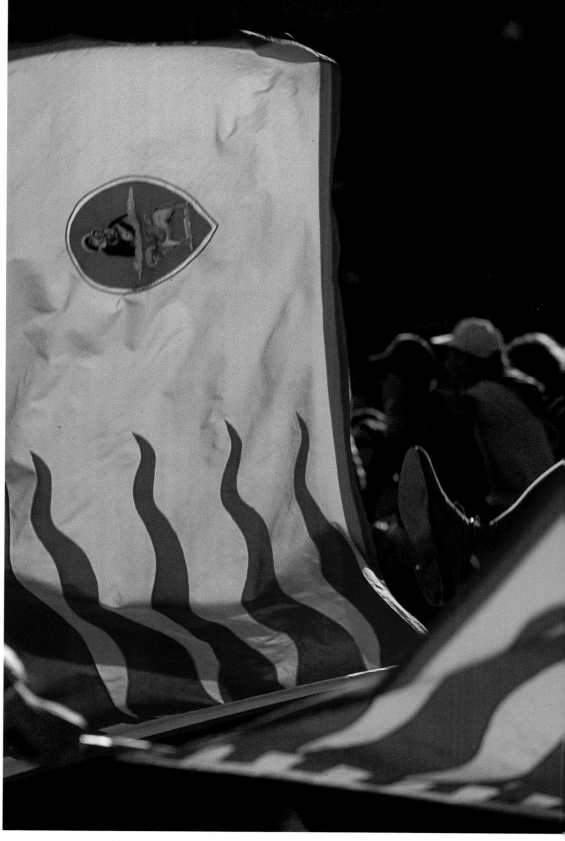

298 left and bottom A splendid procession through the streets of Siena to the Piazza del Campo precedes the Palio. Fourteen groups take part in the procession with a total of 600 people on foot to the sound of drums and trumpets and to the sway of the banners. The costumes are perfect copies of original medieval dress. Each quarter bears its standards which, in the photographs from top to bottom, are of the following quarters: the Dragon, the Wolf, the Goose and the Snail.

298-299 There are seventeen quarters in Siena, symbolized here by flags. Life in each becomes especially animated during the period immediately prior to and after the Palio. Three days before the race the presentation of the horses and practice runs take place. On the eve of the race, the quarters taking part organize huge open air dinners for all their members and their friends.

299 bottom Each jockey wears the symbol of his quarter—in this case a turtle for the quarter of the same name. The horses taking part are treated with maximum care and attention before the race to ensure that they are not interfered with by rival quarters. The competitor is actually the horse and not the rider as a horse may win whether its jockey is still mounted or not.

299 right The Palio of Siena opens with a large historical procession preceded by flag-bearers like those of the Wave (top photograph) or those of Valdimontone (bottom photograph). Their techniques are constantly practiced and handed down from father to son. The reason for such dedication is that the higher the flag reaches, the more advantageous it is to the quarter, but if it should be dropped, bad luck ensues.

300-301 and 300 bottom The Palio at Asti is run on the third Sunday in September and ends a period of festivals started with the Douja d'Or at the beginning of September. The Douja d'Or is the presentation for production of the best wine. At the end of the second week of September, a festival of country cooking takes place with typical local dishes prepared in the piazza by fifty representatives of the Asti province and with parades of local groups in costume. This period is an orgy for lovers of good food and drink. Then come the "propitiatory" dinners in the twenty one quarters and villages that participate in the Palio. When Sunday arrives, a historical procession with 1200 participants in medieval costume takes place. The procession is started by the winning quarter of the previous year's Palio and is followed by all the others. When they arrive in Piazza Alfieri, the Palio begins. First there are the elimination stages, then the final when the horses are ridden bareback.

The Palio in the city of Asti is run on the third Sunday of September. It is a very old festivity which goes back at least to 1275. On the first Saturday of May, the Mayor officially announces the race. Organisation of the event then starts, particularly of the historical procession. On the day of the race, the horses and riders are blessed, each wearing the colors of one of the 14 quarters in the city or of the municipalities round about. The procession starts in the afternoon which involves 300 horses and 1200 people. They wear costumes made from brocade and velvet copied from the miniatures in the 13th century "Codex Astensis" and from the frescoes in the churches. The entire city is in party mood. The colors of the quarter that won the previous year lead the procession. The parade includes the *carroccio,* a large

301 right It was only in 1967 that Asti Palio again took up the tradition that dates back to 1275. This consists of two separate parts: first, the offer of the Palio itself (a bright red sheet of clothe) to the church of San Secondo which takes place on the first Tuesday of May and marks the start of the celebrations in honor of the patron saint of the city; and second, the race itself in September. The race is preceded by propitiatory ceremonies in the parish churches of the city and by a splendid procession in costume from Piazza Cattedrale through the streets of the center to the course. The procession consists of the Carroccio, 100 or so horses and 1200 people wearing the colors of their quarter. There are damsels, knights, pages, armour-bearers, drummers, standard-bearers, flag-bearers, grooms, the Captain of the Palio, officials and the prize-bearers. The race, as in Siena, has no rules— anything goes—the only thing is to win.

301 left The members of the procession wear splendid clothes made from brocade and velvet copied from miniatures in the 13th-century Codex Astensis and from frescoes in the churches. Utmost care is taken in the reproduction of these costumes: every little detail must be correct so as to make the event as representative as possible. The procession is not just a bit of folklore but celebrates some of Asti's proudest historical moments. The Palio at Asti, like that in Siena, attracts a large number of tourists.

farm cart pulled by pairs of oxen, on which the standard of the city is displayed, and a bell, the Martinella, is carried whose tones mark the marching rhythm of the warriors. The riders that take part in the race are often those who race in the Palio of Siena; they ride bareback and without spurs using only bridles, reins and knees to guide the horses. The race is made up of six knockout rounds and a final. The winning horses from each round compete in the final around a course of 460 yards in Piazza Alfieri.

302 bottom left and right In November 1974, a group of Venetians, that already organized a regatta for six-oared boats, met on the island of Burano on the feast day of St. Martin to give life to a unique, noncompetitive rowing event for any type of boat provided it was powered by oars. The event has met with such success each year that now there are more than 3,000 participants from all over the world. The course starts at Bacino San Marco and passes by Burano, Mazzorbo, Madonna del Monte and San Giacomo in Paludo; it then enters Murano via the island's own Grand Canal and heads for Venice. It passes Cannaregio, works its way down the Grand Canal and ends at the Customs in front of St. Mark's.

302 top left and 303 The Venice Regatta, as it has been called since 1889, is held on the first Sunday of September (the name comes from the word remigata meaning a rowing race). The first regatta was held on the Grand Canal on 16 September 1274. Now it is Venice's great festival when the inhabitants hang cloths, tapestries and damasks out on the balconies and roof-terraces along the Canal to welcome the many unusual boats in the procession, among which are the Bucintoro and the Bissona. Today the Regatta culminates with the race of the two-oared gondolas although at one time galleys with twenty or fifty oars participated. On arrival at Ca' Foscari, the winners receive a multicolored banner and the last a booby prize of a suckling pig.

304 top On the second Sunday of May in Camogli, the "Padellata" (padella meaning pan) takes place, a large festival dedicated to fish. The festival has its origin with a vow made on a terrible night during World War II when a group of youths, who had gone out to sea to fish, entered an area planted with mines. Nevertheless they were able to return to land without damage and with their nets full. The local population were so grateful that they decided to offer their entire catch of a night and a day to St. Fortunato once a year.

304 bottom The festival of Corpus Domini usually falls in June and is celebrated with processions across Italy. It is not unusual for whole streets to be decorated with carpets of flowers, the "Infiorat"e, as in this example in the center of Diano Marina. All the road to be covered by the procession becomes a carpet of bright colors in different patterns.

304-305 and 305 bottom left On the night before the feast, bonfires burn on the beach as the villagers wait for the boats to return to port. In the morning an enormous pan measuring more than 13 feet in diameter is brought to the port's square. This is used to fry the two tons of newly caught fish which

are then offered to the spectators as a sign of prosperity. When the fish is offered, the saying is "San Fortunato, pesce regalato" (St. Fortunato, a fish offered) and it is believed that whoever eats this fish will have peace and prosperity all year. The festival closes with a procession and a firework display.

305 top right On the first Sunday in August, the same town of Camogli honors the Stella Maris which corresponds to the Madonna, protectress of sailors and all those on the sea. The procession of boats decorated with holy markings makes its way from Camogli and Punta Chiappa where there is an image of the Madonna. In the darkness, the colored lights make an attractive sight as they are reflected in the water.

305 bottom right On the evening of 14 August in Lavagna, the festival of the Fieschi is held. A cake weighing 1.5 tons commemorates the marriage in 1230 of Count Opizzo Fieschi to Bianca de Bianchi, a noblewoman from Siena, when the event was celebrated by the donation of a huge cake to the local population. Today the festival ends with a procession in 13th-century costume with medieval music and dancing.

306 top, center and 306-307 The festival of St. Ephysus has been celebrated in Cagliari on May 1st each year since 1657. In that year the inhabitants of the city made a vow that they would honor the saint with an annual festival if he caused the plague to halt. The event is especially dear to the hearts of the inhabitants of the quarter of Stampace where the church dedicated to the saint stands. It was built over a prison in which, it is said, he was shut up before being put to death on the order of Diocletian. An effigy of the saint is clothed in formal dress—a white cloak lined with red damask, a blue ribbon on his shoulder, a sash decorated with votive offerings, jewels, necklaces and rings—and hoisted onto an old white coach painted with gold lacquer. He is then led down the streets by thousands of people in multicolored costumes from all parts of Sardinia accompanied by the notes of three-reed flutes. When the procession reaches the church in the nearby village of Giorgino, the saint's sumptuous clothes are changed for more common ones and his statue is placed on a farm cart. The following morning the procession goes to Nora where it remains the whole day. It then returns to Cagliari with the original clothes and in the painted carriage to end the celebrations on May 25th.

306 bottom and 307 top Processions are a feature of the Christian world and are particularly popular in Sardinia where old traditions are an integral part of popular culture. The procession commemorating the crucifixion of Jesus takes place on Good Friday in Alghero (top) and Castelsardo (bottom) with the participation of many local religious houses.

307 center The Sardinian Cavalcade takes place in Sassari on the penultimate Sunday of May.

This is a large parade to commemorate a victory by the Sardinian and Pisan forces over the Arabs in the year 1000. Groups from across the island thread through the streets of the city in a dazzle of colorful costumes. Roughly 3,000 people take part, all in beautiful traditional costumes from the various areas of Sardinia, differing in their shape, materials, ornaments and colors. The principal characters are the knights in costume with their beribboned horses who take part in the parade in the morning and

in the afternoon challenge each other in races and daring tricks. In the late afternoon, groups meet in Piazza Italia to dance and sing. The festival ends, naturally, with banquets in the evening.

307 bottom The Mamuthunes are the main characters in the Carnival at Mamoiada. The origins of these figures are very old and the dances that they perform with their faces hidden by wooden masks are a mixture of archaic and pagan meanings.

308 bottom left, 308 right, 308-309 To celebrate the day of St. John on 24 June, in Florence a type of football match is played in costume. The match is preceded by a parade from the cloister of Santa Maria Novella to Piazza Santa Croce. Mace-bearers, trumpeters, sergeants and the referee take part; behind them come heralds, flag-wavers, musicians and, finally, the drovers with the calf which will be offered to the winners. The four teams taking part wear various outfits and are each composed of 27 players. The goal is a stake covered with cloth and topped by a net. The ball can be pushed with the hands or feet and wrestling is allowed. When the ball passes the stake, the team wins a shot or a point.

308 top left On Easter Sunday in Florence, the "burning of the cart" takes place. It is taken around the city by trumpeters of the city council to be burned in front of the cathedral during Easter mass. The cart looks like a black pyramid decorated with ribbons, frills and flowers and has had this appearance since 1764. The event takes place to commemorate the participation of Pazzino de' Pazzi, from the rich family of Florentine merchants, on the first Crusade to the Holy Land.

309 bottom left The Regatta of the Marine Republics attracts thousands of visitors to Pisa every year. The regatta on the river Arno is actually a historical commemoration but tends to turn into a boat race due to the rivalry between the teams taking part. The event is noted for its rich costumes and the competitiveness between the youths of Pisa, Venice, Genoa and Amalfi.

309 bottom right The Luminaria of St. Rainier takes place at Pisa on 17 June. Rainier was a lay brother who spent time in the Holy Land as a hermit, then lived in Pisa in a monastery. When he died he was buried in the cathedral. On the evening before the saint's day, a procession takes place of his reliquaries accompanied by thousands of wax lamps enclosed in glass beakers which light up the faces of the palazzi along the Arno and are reflected in the river. The four quarters of the city—Sant'Antonio, Santa Maria, San Francesco and San Martino—take part by racing rowing boats on the river. Each boat has eight oarsmen, a cox and a "climber"; he is called this because the winner has to attach his banner to the top of a pole 32 feet high and placed on a boat anchored in the middle of the river by climbing a hawser. The celebrations finish on the last Sunday of the month with the "bridge game": a hundred or so people divided in two teams in the middle of a bridge attempt to push a small cart to the opposing team's bank.

Religious processions are a feature of the whole of the Christian world. There are all sorts, from the most humble in small villages to the choreographed splendors in large cities or places with religious traditions. Routine processions are timed to take place on particular holy days while others are tied to particular circumstances and have to be authorized by the local bishop. Whatever type of procession it is, whether unpretentious or a large festive display, the same rules have to be obeyed: the cross must lead followed by members of the fraternity and clergy; the more important members of these stay close to the officiator who holds up the ostensory and walks in front of the holy image. Many such processions take place at Easter which is often celebrated with sacred representations that involve whole

villages. Beyond its religious significance, processions are a collective ceremony that represent an occasion for universal participation of members of a religious community and the public. Processions in ancient times were often linked to sacred ceremonies but in Rome there were also marriage and funerary processions. Two others were of great importance: the first was for the opening of the circus games when the parade started at the Campidoglio and ended at the Circus Maximus. It was led by a official on a cart and followed by youths, charioteers, athletes and priests bearing images of the gods. The second was the *pompa triumphalis* to celebrate the triumph of a victorious general who was borne on a cart to the temple of Jove Capitolinus, followed by officials, priests, officers and their followers from the defeated army, and by his own soldiers who jeered at the vanquished.

310-311 During the first ten days of June in Val Badia, the festival of the Holy Heart of Jesus is celebrated. Everyone dresses up in the local costume for the procession: the characteristic features of the costume of the musicians is the joppe, a thick jacket of red or brown loden, and

a green felt hat. Children wear crowns of flowers and married women a decorated apron and black lace head-covering. During the ceremony, the statues and traditional standards are carried on shoulders along paths and through fields around the village. Besides its centuries old traditions

preserved by the area's geographical isolation, Val Badia offers spectacular views. Colfosco, Corvara and La Villa, the main centers of the valley, are famous holiday resorts at the feet of the Dolomite mountains, in wide, green airy valleys of extraordinary beauty.

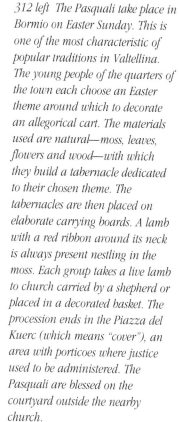

312 left The Pasquali take place in Bormio on Easter Sunday. This is one of the most characteristic of popular traditions in Valtellina. The young people of the quarters of the town each choose an Easter theme around which to decorate an allegorical cart. The materials used are natural—moss, leaves, flowers and wood—with which they build a tabernacle dedicated to their chosen theme. The tabernacles are then placed on elaborate carrying boards. A lamb with a red ribbon around its neck is always present nestling in the moss. Each group takes a live lamb to church carried by a shepherd or placed in a decorated basket. The procession ends in the Piazza del Kuerc (which means "cover"), an area with porticoes where justice used to be administered. The Pasquali are blessed on the courtyard outside the nearby church.

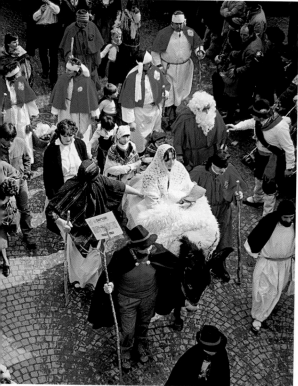

312 top right and 313 Every May the Procession of the Rosario Fiorito is held in Alagna in Valsesia. All the village's inhabitants wear traditional costume and follow a long path through meadows carrying the statue of the Madonna and the standards of the village.

312 center and bottom right The baptism ceremony in Fobello has maintained its ancient medieval rite in which nature and religion are mixed. Dressed in local costume, the godmother carries the baby in its cot over her head from the baby's home to the church. The covering over the cot bears the traditional message, "Nature smiles through her flowers, God through our children."

314 right With the Tiro della Balestra that takes place on the last Sunday of May, the Corsa dei Ceri (Candle Race) is the main folkloric event in Gubbio. It is held in mid-May and is dedicated to St. Hubald, the patron saint of the city and of builders.

314-315 The Corsa dei Ceri takes place in Gubbio on 15 May and is dedicated to St. Hubald, patron saint of the city and of builders. The Ceri are three gigantic wooden constructions, 16 feet high and each weighing 900 lbs. They are made of two octagonal prisms topped by statues of St. Hubald, St. George and St. Anthony Abate. The Ceri are raised in the morning: each team leader jumps up on the stretcher that supports his Cero and pours a jugful of water over the attachment point, the jug is then thrown into the air. The bits of the broken jug are collected by the crowd and kept as good luck tokens.

314 top left The two most important folklore celebrations in Gubbio are the "Tiro della Balestra," on the last Sunday of May, and the "Corsa dei Ceri," dedicated to St. Hubald, that takes place in the middle of the month.

314 bottom left The splendid old town center of Sulmona and the high mountains lining the Peligna valley in Abruzzo are the setting for the procession of a heavy Baroque statue of the Virgin Mary. The statue is carried by eight running men at the culmination of the festival of the "Madonna that Flees in the Square."

315 bottom left On the first day of May in Cocullo, the procession of the Serpari, dedicated to St. Dominic, takes place. Grass snakes placed on the statue of the saint curl around his head and clothes and, according to tradition, are miraculously tamed.

315 bottom right A rather special procession is held in Sulmona during Holy Week. Having learnt of the resurrection of her son Jesus, the Madonna begins to run down the street, losing the black veil that covers her face. At the end of the ceremony, a flock of doves is let loose and the bells are rung.

317 left At San Fratello in the province of Messina, the Abballu di li Giudei is held during Holy Week. Jews are represented in the procession wearing a red muslin jacket and trousers with stripes of different colors, rough leather shoes and a pair of gaiters. Their heads are covered by a mask made of the same muslin with a long, shiny tongue hanging down, long eyebrows and an ugly mouth which give them a diabolical appearance. They carry large link chains which they shake in the faces of the public and a trumpet slung over a shoulder. For the whole of the Thursday and Friday before Easter, they can be found throughout the town, popping out from every corner, climbing on the town walls and making a loud din intermixed with shouts, military marches and musical motifs. These "demons" were originally anti-Semitic representations of Jews, whom early Christians blamed for Christ's death.

316-317 and 316 bottom The Passion and death of Christ are commemorated on the Thursday and Friday before Easter with processions and representations. In the past, dramatized sermons and other ceremonies were held. Today the processions, like this one in Enna on Good Friday, are serious and solemn with the presence of confradies, the local brotherhoods. The rhythm of the processions are marked by the sound of a large drum, the tabbala.

317 right At Adrano in the province of Catania, the Diavolata takes place at Easter. This is a representation, like the one at San Fratello, that has its origin in an antipathy toward the Jews who were thought responsible for the death of Christ. The show takes place on a stage divided into Heaven and Hell; five devils headed by Lucifer argue with Death, with the Soul (a young girl), and with an Angel (a young boy). In the end, it is the young boy that saves humanity by forcing the devils to say the words "Viva Maria" (Long live Mary).

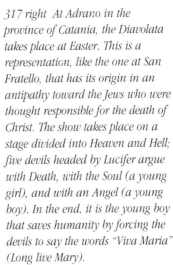

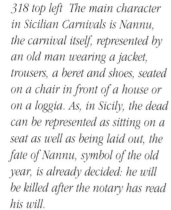

318 center left and bottom Agrigento is mostly known for the battle on 15 May 1860 in which Garibaldi defeated the Bourbon troops but, at Calatafimini nearby, it is also where the Crucifix festival takes place, one of Sicily's most curious festivals. It also goes by the name of Di li Schetti and features a parade of men dressed in black and carrying rifles. The parade exalts the "heroic" aspect of many Sicilian festivals and shows traces of the many and different cultural influences Sicily has assimilated over the centuries.

318 top left The main character in Sicilian Carnivals is Nannu, the carnival itself, represented by an old man wearing a jacket, trousers, a beret and shoes, seated on a chair in front of a house or on a loggia. As, in Sicily, the dead can be represented as sitting on a seat as well as being laid out, the fate of Nannu, symbol of the old year, is already decided: he will be killed after the notary has read his will.

318 right and 318-319 Carnival in Sicily, like this one in Acireale and Mezzojuso, starts on the day of St. Anthony Abate, protector of animals and fire. From this day on, rituals are performed which attempt to distance the negative events of the farming year just ending which might threaten the imminent sprouting of the corn. The different forms of this Carnival are a hangover from the rites used to celebrate mythological gods connected with corn in ancient times, such as Attis, Isis, Adonis, Ceres and Proserpina.

319 bottom One of the most widespread forms of entertainment at a popular level is the puppet theater. The skills of the puppet masters make this a real art form. The shows, generally recounting heroic exploits, are held in theaters in front of loyal and enthusiastic audiences. The characters are nearly always taken from the paladins of France whose deeds are told in the Song of Roland. The public becomes completely involved in the action welcoming or showing disapproval on the appearance of each character. The audience either loves or hates them depending on the role they are playing and on whether the characters conduct themselves according to the rules of behaviour considered correct. When Angelica appears, the audience shouts "bella, bella" as though she were a real actress, whereas the traitor meets with no sympathy at all.

Il più bel Carneva di Sicilia

320 *Italian flags flutter in the breeze on the tower of the Campidoglio in Rome. This special day commemorates the founding of the Eternal City which tradition—with the support of archaeological research—has fixed on April 21st, 753 BC.*

319

REFERENZE FOTOGRAFICHE

Antonio Attini / Archivio White Star: pages 8, 26 top, 26-27, 28 top left, 28-29, 29 center and bottom, 34 top, 70-71, 72, 73, 75, 114 center right, 120 top, 121 top, 197 top and center, 198 bottom, 199, 200, 201 center left, 256 right, 262 top right, 264 top, 264-265.

Marcello Bertinetti / Archivio White Star: pages 1, 6-7, 16 left and bottom, 19 bottom, 20-21, 22 bottom, 22-23, 26 bottom, 27 center and bottom, 33 bottom, 36-37, 38, 38-39, 39 top right, 40-41, 42-43, 44-45, 45 bottom, 46-47, 52, 52-53, 53 bottom left, 54, 55, 56 bottom, 56-57, 57 top and center, 58-59, 60, 61, 67 center, 70 bottom, 71 top right, 80 left, 80 top, 80-81, 81 bottom, 82-83, 86, 96 bottom right, 108 top, 108-109, 140 bottom, 140-141, 141 center top left, 141 center right, 144 left, 144-145, 145 right, 146-147, 148 bottom, 152 top, 152-153, 157 top, 160 top and bottom, 162 top, 170, 171, 172-173, 174 top and center, 175 bottom right, 177 right, 178 top right, 179 center, 184 bottom, 185, 196 top right, 197 bottom, 198-199, 201 top left, 202-203, 203 top, 228 bottom, 229 top and bottom, 232 bottom, 233 right, 234-235, 235, 236, 237, 238-239,

center, 49 bottom right, 50, 51, 53 bottom right, 64 top and center, 64-65, 68 bottom, 69 top right and left, 69 bottom right, 76, 77, 78-79, 80 bottom right, 100 center and bottom, 101 top 102-103, 104, 105, 106, 107, 108 bottom, 109, 110, 111, 112, 113, 114 center left, 115 top, 116-117, 118, 119, 120 center right, 120-121, 122, 123, 124 bottom, 125, 126 top, 126-127, 127 top and center, 128 bottom, 129, 130 center left, 130 bottom, 132 bottom, 133, 134, 135, 136-137, 138, 139, 141 top, 141 center bottom left, 141 bottom, 142, 143, 145 bottom, 148-149, 149, 150 top and bottom, 150-151, 151 bottom, 152 center left and bottom, 153 bottom, 154, 155, 156 right, 156-157, 157 center and bottom, 159, 160-161, 161 top, 162-163, 163 bottom, 164 top and bottom, 164-165, 168 right, 169, 174 bottom left, 174-175, 175 bottom left, 176-177, 177 left, 178 top left, 178-179, 179 top and bottom, 182 bottom left, 182 right, 196-197, 202 top, 203 bottom, 204, 205, 206 top left, 206 bottom right, 206-207, 207 bottom, 208, 209, 210 top, 211, 214, 216, 217, 218 top, 219 top and center, 220, 221 top, 222 top right, 222-223, 223 center and bottom, 224 bottom, 224-225, 225 top left, 225 bottom right, 226 bottom left, 246 top, 246-247, 247 center and bottom, 248 top, 249 center and bottom, 250, 251, 252 bottom, 253 top, 254, 256 left, 256-257, 257 bottom, 263, 266, 268, 269 left, 270 top, 271, 272, 273, 278, 279, 281 top, 282, 283, 284, 285, 286, 287, 288, 289 top, 292, 293, 306, 307, 308, 308-309, 309 bottom left, 312 center right, 313, 314 top and center, 314-315, 316, 317, 318, 319.

Anne Conway: pages 300, 301.

Stefano Amantini / Atlantide: pages 120 center left, 252 top, 252-253, 255.

M. Amendola / Franca Speranza: page 120 bottom.

Giulio Andreini: page 295 top and bottom.

Archivio Scala: pages 194, 195, 212, 213, 218-219, 219 bottom, 223 top, 258, 259, 260, 261, 264 bottom, 265 top, 267, 270 bottom, 274 bottom, 275 center.

Franco Barbagallo: pages 30 center, 30-31, 128 top, 130 top, 130 center right, 130-131, 131 bottom, 132-133, 150 center.

Foto Benini / Really Easy Star: page 161 bottom.

F. Bertuzzi / SIE: page 302 top left.

Attilio Boccazzi Varotto: page 201 bottom left, 201 right.

Massimo Borchi / Atlantide: pages 124-125.

Cameraphoto: pages 86-87, 87 top, 226 right, 227, 233 left, 234 bottom, 303.

Foto Cautillo: pages 127 bottom, 280 top and bottom.

Elio and Stefano Ciol: pages 274-275, 275 top and bottom, 276, 277.

Anne Conway: pages 300, 301.

Guido Cozzi / Atlantide: pages 33 top, 232-233.

Giovanni Dagli Orti: pages 190 top, 190 bottom right.

Araldo De Luca: pages 12, 13, 174 bottom right, 183, 186, 187, 190 bottom left, 191, 192-193.

Farabola Foto: page 206 top right.

FMR: pages 220-221.

Franco Furoncoli: page 247 top.

Cesare Gerolimetto: pages 14-15, 27 top, 162 bottom, 176 bottom, 180-181, 184-185.

Gräfenhaim / Sime: page 225 bottom left.

Granata Press Service: page 74.

I. G. D. A.: page 249 top.

Nippon TV: pages 188 bottom, 188-189, 189 bottom.

Pessina / Really Easy Star: page 168 top left.

Guido Rossi / The Image Bank: pages 88-89, 225 top right.

Giovanni Simeone / Marka: page 165 bottom.

Giovanni Simeone / SIE: pages 161 center, 222 top and left, 269 bottom right.

Giovanni Simeone / Sime: pages 2-3, 10-11, 43 top and bottom left, 48-49, 49 top and bottom left, 84, 85, 88 top, 166, 167, 206 bottom left, 210 bottom, 215, 228-229, 229 center, 230-231, 269 top right.

A. Tradii: pages 248-249.

Giulio Veggi: pages 70 top, 71 top left.

240, 241, 242 top, 243 bottom, 245 top, 262 top left, 262-263, 280-281, 288-289, 294 top, 294-295, 295 center, 296, 297, 298, 299, 302 bottom left, 302 right, 304, 304-305, 305 bottom left, 309 bottom right, 312 left, 312 top and bottom right, 320.

Anne Conway / Archivio White Star: pages 32 left, 90, 91, 92, 93, 94-95, 96 bottom left, 96-97, 97, 98, 99, 100 top, 100-101, 168 bottom right, 242-243, 243 top, 244-245, 244 bottom, 245 center and bottom, 305 top and bottom.

Luciano Ramires / Archivio White Star: pages 22 top and center, 24 top and bottom, 24-25, 25 top left, 39 top left, 43 right, 44 top and bottom, 49 top right, 57 right, 62, 63, 64 bottom, 65 bottom, 66 top and bottom , 66-67, 67 bottom, 68-69, 69 bottom left, 89, 114 top, 114 bottom, 114-115, 290, 291, 310, 311, 314 bottom, 315 bottom.

Giulio Veggi / Archivio White Star: pages 4-5, 9, 14 bottom, 15 top and bottom, 16-17, 18 top, 18-19, 19 top, 25 top right, 28 top right, 29 top, 30 top and bottom, 32-33, 33 center, 34 center and bottom, 34-35, 36, 42 top, 44

AIR CONCESSIONS

Concession S. M. A. No. 1-634 of 04/11/1997; Concession S. M. A. No. 949 of 19/11/1993; Concession S. M. A. No. 12-121 of 20/09/1994; Concession S. M. A. No. 126 of 18/04 /1995; Concession S. M. A. 12-180 of 11/11/1994; Concession S. M. A. No. 316 of 18/08/1995; Concession Aeronautica Militare R. G. S. No. 1-456 of 20/07/1998; Concession S. M. A. No. 1-480 of 28/10/1996; Concession S. M. A. No. 493 of 28/05/1998; Concession S. M. A. No. 31-023 of 09/08/1994; Concession S. M. A. No. 31-027 of 11/08/1994; Concession S. M. A. No. 31-017 of 08/08/1994; Concession S. M. A. No. 31-022 of 09/08/1994; Concession S. M. A. No.31-026 of 08/08/1994.